A GROOM
OF ONE'S
OWN

A Groom of One's Own

and Other Bridal Accessories

MIMI POND

A DUTTON BOOK

DUTTON
Published by the Penguin Group
Penguin Books USA Inc., 375 Hudson Street,
New York, New York 10014, U.S.A.
Penguin Books Ltd, 27 Wrights Lane,
London W8 5TZ, England
Penguin Books Australia Ltd, Ringwood,
Victoria, Australia
Penguin Books Canada Ltd, 2801 John Street,
Markham, Ontario, Canada L3R 1B4
Penguin Books (N.Z.) Ltd, 182-190 Wairau Road,
Auckland 10, New Zealand
Penguin Books Ltd, Registered Offices:
Harmondsworth, Middlesex, England
First published by Dutton, an imprint of New American
Library, a division of Penguin Books USA Inc.
Distributed in Canada by McClelland & Stewart Inc.
First Printing, June, 1991
10 9 8 7 6 5 4 3 2 1
Copyright © Mimi Pond, 1991
All rights reserved

REGISTERED TRADEMARK—MARCA REGISTRADA

Library of Congress Cataloging-in-Publication Data:
Pond, Mimi
    A groom of one's own, and other bridal accessories /
Mimi Pond.
      p.   cm.
    ISBN 0-525-24997-4
    1. Weddings—United States—Planning. 2. Betrothal—
United States. 3. II: Better classed in HQ801, PN
(Humor); BJ   (etiquette); GT (Manners and customs).
—awk [fh08] I. Title.
HQ745.P66   1991
395'.22—dc20   90-26037
                                                    CIP

Printed in the United States of America
Set in Goudy Old Style
Designed by Barbara Huntley

*This book is dedicated to the man
who made it all possible: my husband,
Wayne White*

Acknowledgments

Because truth is stranger than fiction, this book would not have been possible without the true stories and astute observations of my very funny, articulate, and expressive friends. Monumental thanks to:

Erica Buchsbaum, Chris Connelly, Lucy Cook, Jay Cotton, Liza and Alan Cranis, Sarah Ebling, Susan Fitzpatrick, Jean Flynn and Bobby Pollard, Bill Franzen, Sarajo Frieden, Ellen Fuchs, Tony Gardner, Sally Govan, Melanie Graham, Brian Griffin and Amy Neff, Matt Groening, Lianne Halfon, Al Jean and Mike Reiss, Phyllis Katz, Nancy Kintisch, Lisa Stewart Keating, Stephen Kroninger and Aviva Ebstein, Gary Luke, Dick Lynn and Judy Minot, Tom and Melissa Mitchell, Monty Montgomery, Melinda Moore, Alison Mork, Barbara O'Dair, Gary Panter, Steve Parrott, Mary Peacock, Mike Quinn and Priscilla Van Tries, Candy Rinehart, Robin Sagon, Bill Sensing, Ann Shields, Molly Shields, Mireille Soria, Ellen Stern, Lynne Stewart, and Mim Udovitch.

Extra special thanks to my parents, whose love, generosity of spirit, and common sense really did make my wedding The Most Beautiful Day of My Life.

Contents

1 A GROOM OF ONE'S OWN

"Honey, I'm home!"

WHAT DOES IT MEAN when suddenly you find yourself dreaming of a smiling man in a suit who carries a briefcase and a bunch of daisies? There's only one kind of man like that who floats into the collective dreamscape of American women. It's a *husband*. That's it! Yes, you'd like one of those. It's a revelation that, even once you've owned up to it, seems . . . well, too grownup for words. Embarrassing. You're too young, too hip, too swinging and wild to be called someone's *wife*. And yet you feel an undeniable urge to call your boyfriend *hubby*. In fact, you crave a lifestyle that once seemed to you as outdated as the *Donna Reed Show*. And be honest—you kind of dig Donna. Worse still, Ricky Ricardo, Ozzie Nelson—even Carl Betz (Mr. Donna Reed)—are beginning to look kind of, well, *sexy* in those late-night reruns. Reruns you watch, now that you no longer have to comb the dark side streets for a man. Once you realize you can actually picture that guy at your side in pajamas, you'll know you've finally found your very own Ward Cleaver. And isn't that your theme music now?

Popping the Question

So maybe it didn't happen the way you dreamed it—him on his knees, or him handing you a glass of champagne with your engagement ring in it, or the both of you on top of the Eiffel Tower, or in a gondola on the Grand Canal, or any of those romantic things. Quite possibly it happened more like this, one night during a lull on the *Carson Show*.

HER: Well?

HIM: Well what?

HER: Well, are we going to talk about it?

HIM: Talk about what?

HER: You know what.

HIM: (exasperated) What?

HER: Getting married.

HIM: (long silence).

HER: Well?

HIM: I told you. I don't want to talk about it.

HER: You always say that.

HIM: What's there to say?

HER: Well, do you want to or not?

HIM: You want to get married?

HER: I asked you first.

HIM: No, do *you* want to.

HER: Of course *I* do, you idiot.

HIM: No, I'm *asking* you. Do you want to get married?

HER: Is that a proposal? Is that what you call a proposal?

HIM: All right. *Will* you marry me?

HER: Sure.

Sure. You know when not to push a good thing too far. Then you snuggle a little closer and nei-

ther one of you says another word, while tears of joy glisten in your eyes. No matter where he asks you to be his girl forever, it's bound to be a moving moment—but did you ever think that your life would change while Johnny was making jokes about Joan Embry's baboon?

From here on in, nothing will ever be the same. Like being pregnant, there's no such thing as being just a little bit engaged.* Everyone will begin to treat you differently. Not just your family and friends, but total strangers. Try this experiment. When someone you do casual business with—say, your dry cleaner—asks you how you're doing, mention that you're getting married. Tears will well up in his or her eyes. He or she will take your hand and either pump it fiercely or pat it fondly. "Congratulations," your dry cleaner will say,

*Even if your engagement is broken later on, you in no way ever revert back to the wild, carefree, single lifestyle you used to lead. Instead, you become That Girl with the Broken Engagement. Try, for the sake of others, to look haunted.

"and God bless." Remember: People you *don't even know* want to see you settled. But don't expect a discount.

The first strange thing that happens is that your boyfriend becomes your *fiancé*. Now, there's no faster way of sounding like a complete twit than when using this word, especially around co-workers, friends, and family. Even tossing the "f" word off casually, you begin to think of yourself as an aging ingenue, an over-the-hill That Girl. You'll notice that your husband-to-be will find ways to avoid referring to you in public as *his* fiancée. When questioned about his resistance, he'll say it's because using French words make him sound—well, like a sissy. Never mind. You'll accompany your *fiancé* to talk to the minister, go with your *fiancé* to get your marriage license, shop for rings with your *fiancé*—and that's just for starters. You've never felt more like a grownup in your life. When you actually begin to plan your wedding together, it will set the tone for all the other truly adult rites of passage that you go through together as a married couple—like buying a house, having children, or shopping for a sump pump at WalMart.

Romancing the Stone

We would like our fiancés to be worshipful fools who shower us with diamonds, rubies, and pearls—but that doesn't always happen. If we truly adore

them, we don't have unrealistic romantic expectations. We love them for all the wonderful things we have in common—a respect for the same ideals, a sharing of the same hopes and dreams—and most importantly—the capacity to ignore one another's repellent personal grooming habits. Still, we would like to have a, well, a little romantic something to symbolize our impending vows. We just would. Unfortunately for us, prostate surgery is more attractive to a great many men than shopping. Now, if we wanted a table saw or a set of shocks to symbolize a promise of lifetime commitment, it might be a different story—but they'd just as soon weasel out of this ring business. Besides, they know that we hip, independent, nineties kind of gals are too proud to beg for this niggling, square-cut or pear-cut little detail. And that's where they get us. Every woman knows that whining for your own engagement ring is considered unattractive and rude. Still, men must be set straight. We could drop hints, but that's too much like begging. More insidious methods work better—his female relatives, for example. Getting a sympathetic sister, mother, or aunt to shame him into submission can work much more effectively and attractively. Even if female relatives are not available, he is bound to cave in eventually. At every social event that we attend where we announce our engagement, we can count on our own sex to squeal with delight and demand to see the ring. When we innocently

say, "Why, I don't have one," all betrayal-filled eyes will turn to Him.

The general rule of thumb about how much money should be spent on an engagement ring is two months' salary. Just whose rules and thumbs *are* these? Why, some crafty jewelers' association, of course. If you're engaged to an investment banker, this means you've got a pretty substantial rock coming your way. But what if your special guy has yet to realize his money-earning potential—that is to say, what if he's the assistant beverage manager of a Carl's Jr? Beware these two nightmare-inducing words: cubic zirconia. Face it. Cubic zirconia is the Ginzu knife of the gemstone world, appearing twenty-four hours a day on Home Shopping Club TV screens the world over. For a tiny percentage of what the Real Thing costs, your minimum-wage slave of love figures he can get you something even Zsa-Zsa Gabor would consider too flashy. It doesn't matter that most people can't tell the real from the phony. With someone like you wearing over a carat—not to mention four—everyone will know that your fiancé was overwhelmed by romance, a ponypack of Bud Light, *and* the thrill of getting a "toot" from Tootie, the Home Shopping Club mascot. Suggest a visit to a reputable jeweler who will obsequiously manipulate your beloved into paying through the nose for a microchip-sized gemstone. This way, all your girlfriends can squeal and squint at the same time.

Telling the World

Savor this moment. This is the time to enjoy and daydream about just how wonderful it's all going to be. Your new engagement ring becomes a vehi-

cle to tell the big news to everyone, even strangers—the bus driver, the checkout clerk at the store, that gal in the next stall. You're walking on air, adrift in a dream, awash in a world of love—until you discover that just the word "wedding" does something to people. You need only to mention the happy event once or twice for everyone you know to presume an invitation is in the mail, and that yelling "best wishes" across a crowded room is an RSVP. And that's where your heartache begins. From here on out, it's a downward spiral of anxiety, bad dreams, bickering, budgeting, price lists, guest lists, estimates, arguments, abuse, and three-way mirrors.

You thought you were pretty hip, pretty with-it, pretty darned sophisticated. You thought you had seen it all—after all. You lived through the sexual revolution and the Me Decade. You pogoed and slam-danced with the best of them. Maybe you even got a tattoo or an unorthodox part of your body pierced. Well, nothing you ever did before is going to prepare you for what you have to do now. Once you've made the decision to get

married and plan a wedding—even if you're tying the knot on top of a Mayan pyramid—you'll find yourself caught up in rites of passage especially designed to make you feel more square than Debbie Boone.

Wedding Manual Labor

You'll be looking for guidance, of course. Today's wedding etiquette and style books insist that there is no reason why your Big Day, no matter how small, can't have the same éclat as Charles and Diana's. The pictures show elegant people, sumptuous settings, exquisite foods. But not a single picture in these books seems to relate to anything that is likely to happen at *your* wedding—because, of course, everyone you know looks like real people. And there's nothing wrong with that. The ones to be suspicious of are the people who *don't* have overweight aunts in pleated floral caftans, grandfathers in powder-blue polyester, and divorced, loud moms in tight, low-cut sheaths. Sure, it may be possible to control the setting and the food at this, your major life event—but don't make the mistake of trying to work makeover magic on your family. Fantasizing that you grew up in a Ralph Lauren magazine spread will only bring you disappointment on your wedding day. After all, your tacky loved ones are precisely the people who will make this day a Wedding, and not just another shallow, meaningless party where you and your tasteful friends have "fun."

There are books to inform you about table settings, books to instruct you on the correct way to write a thank-you note, but there has been nothing, until now, to guide you, the guileless bride-

to-be through the minefield that is bound to be your wedding planning experience. Wedding rules: Sure, you'll learn them. You'll know them. You'll break them. You'll discover that your friends and relatives are capable of inventing their own weird etiquette rules out of thin air.

Made-up etiquette? You may think this is just a lighthearted jest. In these early, halcyon planning stages, you can't imagine everyone not trying their hardest to make things easy for you, the happiest girl on earth. Just wait—when you least expect it, your maid of honor will say, "God, I can't believe you don't know that if your *best friend* is the maid of honor you pay for her dress and her hotel room and her airfare. It's the way it's done." This rule isn't in any bridal book you ever heard of, and

Don't make the mistake of trying to work makeover magic on your family.

9

yet she's dead serious. When imaginary social rules come from family, though, you're really sunk. How do you contradict your aunt-in-law-to-be when she says, "Darling, the maid of honor's escort is *always, always, always* the groom's second cousin—and considering Barton has been de-institutionalized just for the occasion, I think it's the very least we can do for him." Worst of all is when your own grandmother, the last keeper of the etiquette flame, informs you with great authority that the groom's family is responsible for "the flowers in the church, the hors d'oeuvres, tipping the bartender, certain dry-cleaning bills, and at the very least, the *gesture* of offering a downpayment on a home for the newlyweds. Not only that—but if they don't know, it's *your* responsibility to tell them, dear." Begging to differ with Amy Vanderbilt Jr. is out of the question. And don't think you can just ignore these dictums. People that wrapped up in rules will ride you to make sure that things are being done correctly. Don't worry. They don't actually want to see rules followed to the letter. No, for the etiquette-happy, the smug satisfaction is in knowing that others are so socially inferior that there's no hope for them. Don't disappoint them. Lie like crazy and blame everyone else. This is your right as a bride-to-be. Planning your own coming-of-age experience may wither you prematurely, but just think of it this way: If you can get through this, childbirth should be a breeze.

Not for the Shy

If you're one of those unassuming, introverted types—one of those people who finds being in the spotlight just too embarrassing for words—you may find the celebration of your marriage awkward—not to mention sheer torture. If you have given a lot of thought to what's being glorified, it can be pretty darn embarrassing. After all, a wedding is *only* a celebration of the archaic ritual sacrifice of your maidenhead to the member of another tribe. They don't call it a *hymeneal* rite for nothing. Are you blushing yet? Not to worry. What's really being celebrated at a modern wedding is female self-indulgence at its peak—and the acquisition of small, attractive European-designed appliances. Perhaps you should order one of those video assertiveness seminars they offer on late-night television, so you can push your way to the front lines of the bridal battle. Even if you're the most unassuming person you know, as a bride, *you must glory in your moment.* If this is beyond your modest scope, imagine how you'd do things if you were nominated—and sure to win—an Academy Award. No. That's not big enough. Imagine how you'd do things if you became President of the United States. Wait. Better yet, imagine just how you'd do things if you were crowned *Queen of the Whole World.* As Queen of the World, you'd want to look your most fabulous, of course, and you'd definitely want a coronation party, including all your relatives,

*Even if you're the most unassuming
person you know, as a bride,
you must glory in your moment.*

old boyfriends, and their new girlfriends. You've just *got* to look good in front of them. And unless you plan to become an egocentric movie star bitchgoddess, you will never again have the excuse to act like a monster and wear tulle at the same time. It's expected of you. Pull out all the stops.

There are really only two kinds of brides: "A" brides, the kind who have dreamed of a perfect wedding all their lives, and "B" brides, the kind who, up until this moment, have never, ever given one moment's thought to what kind of wedding they'd have. Both are equally likely to fall into traps: "A" simply assumes that her wedding is going to be a riot of stirring pageantry, lace, and bridal cocktail stirrers—just like Charles and Diana's. "B" doesn't have a clue as to what she wants, so she ends up with a wedding *exactly* like "A" 's.

If you are a "B" bride, you'll be shocked to discover suddenly that, yes, you *do* have some very specific ideas. Mostly they're what you definitely don't want, based on what you will see in bridal

"A" simply assumes that her wedding is going to be a riot of stirring pageantry . . .

magazines. The trick is to avoid swans, any Kenny Rogers songs, and matchbooks and napkins with the words ENDLESS LOVE and the bride's and groom's names on them.

Never underestimate the possibility that you are actually an "A" bride disguised as a "B" bride. Sure, you may think that all traditional conditioning forced on you as a child is a thing of the past. Things are different now. After all, you've escaped your middle-class upbringing. You went to Brandeis, you've lived in Greenwich Village for fourteen years, and now you're marrying an artist. How could your wedding possibly be anything but a very groovy, bohemian affair? Well, don't come crying to me when your simple nuptial plans for thirty guests on a barge in the East River turn into an event for three hundred at the midtown Hilton with you in a big ball of tulle. Try, instead, to enjoy what you wanted all along.

You may think these cautionary notes do not apply to you, since you have your own personal

"B" doesn't have a clue.

style that will override traditional stodginess and make your special day a carefree, wonderful affair. Think again. *You have no control.* Elements are at work here far beyond your powers as a mere mortal, a woman, and a bride. Your wedding will not be what you think it is going to be, no matter what you think it is going to be.

The myriad factors that a can put a crimp in your personal style are endless. To start with, there's your wedding timeframe. There's your budget. And then, of course, there's your own bad self. The experience of planning your wedding may bring out a side of you you've never known. And loved ones will be quick to criticize the new you. Pejoratives like "obsessed," "bullying," "fanatic," and "anal retentive" may fill the air. Caution: You may begin to question your own sense of right and wrong. Is your public tantrum over the choice of rented flatware really irrational? What about throwing crockery at the mere suggestion of baby's breath? Okay, well, then, how about if, only weeks before the wedding, Mom wants you to change your wedding date so she can go on that seniors cruise? Would any jury convict you? You'll no longer be sure what's unreasonable anymore. And these just skim the surface of the foreseeable problems. The unknown factors are just that—unexplained by science, triggered by the phases of the moon, the forces of astrology, and the menstrual cycles of many, they will pop up at the most unlikely moments.

So, remember your most important lesson: *You have no control.* And yes, it is hard to express sensitively you and your beloved's oneness with the universe against the backdrop of Swedish meatballs and an all-geriatric band doing a cover of "Cele-

brate" by Kool and the Gang, but remember—other people have been doing it this way for years—and though they didn't have a good time either, no one could deny that they had been to a wedding.

2. THE BIGGEST DRESS IN THE WORLD

A white wedding begins to snowball.

IMPENDING NUPTIALS. It sounds like a stage of reptile reproduction. But now, it's happening to you. Is it any wonder you're confused? The one thing you are sure about is that on your wedding day, you are going to be wearing the most incredible, the most beautiful, the most fabulous dress in the world. Not in *this* world—but in a world within which you'll soon find yourself trapped, a world you never created. It's Wedding World! As soon as you start shopping, you'll find yourself sucked into a kaleidoscope of chantilly lace, polyester satin, and plastic swans. None of this has anything whatsoever to do with your personal identity, your values, or your taste. The whole thing is silly, frivolous—embarrassing, really. On the other hand (the one with that engagement ring *you* insisted on), you're eating it all up. And what girl wouldn't? Society has tattooed "wedding" on our frontal lobes. All those flowers, ribbons, pastels— hey, if you liked it as a baby, you're going to love it as a bride. Mom and Dad shoved the idea down our throats since we were old enough to know our colors. Then they said, "Pick two for your theme." Even if you haven't thought about it since you were five, they're probably the same two pastel shades.

It's never too early to start planning for your dress. Some girls have been drawing it over and over, for as long as they can remember, first in crayon, then on the margins of their class notes, now on the backs of legal pads and business contracts. These gals are prepared. Are you?

The most important thing, of course, is that you should look more stunning than you have ever looked in your life. How many excuses do you have to wear a dress bigger than anyone else's, at a party just for you, where everyone has to burst into tears from how gorgeous you look while you prance

Some girls have been drawing it over and over, for as long as they can remember . . .

around in front of them? Remember, your lifelong happiness depends on this one article of clothing. If it doesn't look good, you're not a bride. You're just some idiot in a big white thing—a color unflattering to about 93 percent of the population. And it's not just your outfit you have to worry about. You have to engineer an entire affair around this dress. This is the one chance you'll get to accessorize yourself with not just a sassy scarf or belt, but a major life event!

Whether you shop for your dress in a classy department store or at a Latino bridal palacio, you've got *sucker* written across your forehead. Those sharks are counting on that "no-expenses-spared-for-the-most-important-day-of-my-life" hysteria. They can see you coming a billion miles away. But hon, if you can't get it on sale, you don't want it. Why not pay a visit to your local mega-giant cut-rate discount designer Bride-O-Rama? The experience will galvanize you. Usually, you'll have to make an appointment weeks, sometimes months in advance. You may even have to drive hundreds of miles to experience this frenzy of prenuptial fever. Dozens of other brides-to-be are there with their entourages—their mother, their sister, their sister's baby, their cousin, their cousin's cute little shitzu (pronounced shit-zoo). These women are whipped up so bad that their estrogen seems to vibrate in the air like negative ions. The atmosphere is more congratulatory than a wide-mouthed bass meet—"Ya landed one! Way to go!" If the grooms-to-be could see their future brides in this light, they'd be having more than just second thoughts.

You'll have signed in. They know your name, but still you will be introduced as "The Bride," the way nurses say to the doctor, "This is The Patient." In other words, you will be treated like someone who is very, very sick. Your disease? Wanting a white dress. Don't worry. They'll humor you. "What is the wedding date?" is the first question you'll be asked. Even if you tell them "June 2001," they'll look horrified, query "Early or late June?" push you into a dressing room, measure your hips, critically eye your breasts, and tell you that they'll have to put in a special rush order. If you suggest the idea that you were thinking of *maybe* not wearing an actual bridal gown, but something a little more, well, you—the saleslady may throw herself at your feet and implore you,

Dozens of other brides-to-be are there with their entourages—their mothers, their sisters, their sisters' babies, their cousins, their cousins' cute little shitzus.

19

"Please, just promise me you won't wear a suit."
Instead of what you asked for, she'll bring in her
top-of-the-line ten-thousand-dollar Carolina Her-
rera and insist that you try it on, just for fun,
just—it seems—to humor *her*. Naturally, once
you've got it on, she'll burst into tears—an excel-
lent sales technique. "Every bride should be a fairy
princess," she'll sob.

Princess *is* the operative word. Here in the bridal
dugout, they're catering to that Disney fairy tale
fantasy they know you've been nurturing since you
were four. Wedding dress style, you'll discover,
exists outside of fashion, in a bridal vacuum. It
bears no relation to real life—unless you call Las
Vegas real. You'll be shown Cher's wedding dress,
Charo's wedding dress, Pia Zadora's wedding dress.
Sequins, pearls, tassels, bugle beads abound. Why,
it's almost operatic—leaning toward the *Grand Old*

"*Every bride should be a
fairy princess,*"
she'll sob.

Opry. Dolly Parton is the only woman on earth who conceivably dresses like this every day. But somehow, in that three-way mirror, you won't favor Dolly. You won't resemble a fairy princess. You'll look more like a cream horn with arms.

The demanding fairy princess lifestyle insists that all these dresses have *huge* puffed sleeves—mandatory, it seems, even for those of us with linebacker shoulders, and so very flattering to short gals with tiny heads. Optical illusions aside, there is something about these gowns that conspires to transform you from someone with a lively personality into a bland icon—a life-size cake ornament, instead of the more fabulous you you imagined. Is there no way around this?

Perhaps the solution is to have your dress custom-made. Don't take up your fabulous seamstress friend's offer to do it. With your luck, she'll have some kind of artistic breakdown over just how ultimate she can make your ultimate wedding dress. You'll have to wear the results, and you'll hate her forever because the most beautiful day of your life wasn't the most beautiful day of your life. Find a professional. That is, if you're capable of expressing yourself without feeling intimidated by someone who's obviously more of a woman that you'll ever be—someone who can really sew.

After logging a few hundred hours in yardage stores, you'll be bandying about terms you never knew existed before—peau de soie, pongee, shantung, Alençon, passamenterie, candy-box bows, bishop sleeves, basque waists, chapel trains. What's more, you can spend just as much money as you would in a bridal boutique, but at least you'll get what you crave—even more random abuse from strangers. Assert yourself with your

dressmaker, or you might end up looking like a cake, a lamp, or a boudoir chair. It's important that you get it right, because you've only got this one shot. Even if you get married again and again, you'll be demoted to somewhere between a The-First-One-Didn't-Count Ivory and the Let's-Not-Kid-Ourselves Navy Blue Suit. Ultimately, it all depends on whether you want people to recognize you—the ultimate, most fabulous you ever, but definitely you—or if you want them to see *The Bridal Gown That Ate Chicago*.

You'll discover your vision of an intimate little gathering will explode now that you've bought that frock. Once you've got a full-length silk organza triple-peplum gown with a beaded embroidery lattice overlay, portrait collar, and moiré cathedral train, you can't just serve a few people sherbet-and-gingerale punch and cake. No, we're suddenly talking sitdown for two hundred, or at least buffet for one hundred and fifty.

And so, with one simple purchase, your wedding has become an epic production. You'll need extras—in wedding lingo, we call them brides-

Someone invented bridesmaids so that all your girlfriends could wear ugly dresses to guarantee that you'll look even prettier.

maids, the backup singers of matrimony. Someone invented them so that all your girlfriends could wear ugly dresses to guarantee that you'll look even prettier. They are proving that good friends are willing to humiliate themselves just for you, on this, your Special Day. Since whatever dress you choose for them will inevitably be ludicrous, why stop at just two or three bridesmaids? You're not paying through the nose for these dresses—they are. Go for twelve, for a monumentally hideous effect. Here's a tip: think gingham. Make them buy the matching hat, gloves, and parasol, too. Tradition demands that you tell them a lie bigger than "the check is in the mail": that they can cut the dress off and wear it again. Custom also permits them to curse your first-born child.

Once you make a dress decision, you'll have second and third thoughts—not about having committed yourself to organizing a social event of a scale you've never dreamed of. Not about a major expenditure that will set back your plans for real

estate investment for the next five years. No. It's what if the dress you've chosen *isn't* absolutely the most fabulously perfect ideal wedding dress of all time? Call your therapist, read deeper shades of meaning into it, but look at it this way—if you can choose one man, you can choose one dress.

Any woman who lived as a single woman through the 1970s may find herself steered toward these shades. Discover the true meaning of "off" white.

almond	bisque	bone
buttercup	camellia	candlelight
champagne	chardonnay	cream
desert sand	ecru	eggshell
ivory	jasmine	natural
oatmeal heather	old lace	oyster
parchment	pearl	rice powder
sea mist	taupe	vanilla
winter wheat		

3 INDUSTRIALIZED WEDDINGS

Show me a woman with a subscription to a bridal magazine and I'll show you someone who doesn't even have a boyfriend.

UNLESS YOU'RE THE KIND of woman who's been dreaming of her wedding day since she was born, you've probably never picked up a bridal magazine before in your life. Sure you've had them thrust at you, open, as friends and co-workers with a hysterical glint in their eyes beg you for your opinion about *their* wedding gowns, but you've never opened one at the newsstand, much less bought any. It always seemed . . . premature before. Anyway, aren't teen trailer brides the only women who actually buy these things? Okay, maybe not, but really, you're way past this. But you've got to start somewhere. When you casually hand it to your local newsstand vendor, like it was just another copy of the *New York Review of Books*, he says loudly, "Preetty lady finally get married? Congradoolations!" Stuff it hurriedly into your purse. At home, wait until there's no one else around to open it up. Draw the shades. Don't worry, it's not porno. But after wading through

reams of ads for wedding stationary, rental limos, personalized rice bags, dyeable shoes, and bridesmaids' dresses that could double as toilet seat covers, you wonder who on earth indulges in a fantasy this estrogen-charged. Why, lots of women. They don't intend for things to end up this way. It's just that . . . well, one bride-to-be put it this way: "Remember when you were eleven years old and you thought how great it would be to get your period? And then you got it? That's what planning a wedding is like."

The tone of some bridal magazines implies that you, as a future married person, are about to enter a mist-enshrouded world of Gracious Living—a world that somehow involves plastic slipcovers and pleated brocade drapes. They suggest that you are about to give up your protracted career as a wild, irresponsible teenager and finally become a respectable, decent, church-going adult. They indicate that the physical process of planning and going through your wedding will be the very thing that transforms you—the nuptials-as-reform-school approach. These magazines also hint that the products they advertise and advocate will speed this process. For most of us, however, just getting married doesn't mean *really* growing up. It just means finally having a blender with a lid, some appropriate barware, and real cereal bowls instead of old Cool Whip containers. Believe me, when you're really grown up—after the kids arrive—you'll serve cocktails in Care Bear cups and not even care.

The bridal magazine business is a racket. It's fairly obvious that 99 percent of all brides-to-be only buy one of these magazines in their life—how else could the publishers get away with publishing the same articles month after month? These are:

- Duties of the members of the wedding party (at which your friends will laugh)
- A guide to men's formal wear (my favorite question—"What are studs?")
- How to buy elaborate china, silver, and crystal (that you won't trot out until your future children marry, when it will all look hopelessly passé)
- Honeymoon travel tips (generally involving pictures of beaches, tropical drinks, and a bad color photo of a Holiday Inn disco that might as well be in Fargo, North Dakota)
- Etiquette column—the "who pays for what" is a real joke, because if the groom's family doesn't know that they're responsible for shelling out anything, who are you to point it out to them, Little Miss Priss?
- New, exciting floral arrangements—that you will show to your florist (who will make up something that looked fashionable in 1963)

As your wedding day grows nearer, you will find yourself in the swirling vortex of a logistical nightmare. This is already obvious to your co-workers, who've been listening to your paranoid ravings that

others are persecuting you *just to ruin your wedding*—doing terrible, mean, spiteful things—like forcing you to do your job. Remember: only those who really love you will tolerate having pages from bridal magazines waved under their noses. Only your closest girlfriends will pretend to listen to you debate the merits of poached vs. grilled salmon. And nobody—really, nobody—cares what song you choose for your first dance, as long as it's not "Once, Twice, Three Times a Lady." Because you've never given a party this size before, you're simply not prepared for just how overwhelming it can all be. In fact, if you're like most of us, you've never thrown an affair that required more than a case of beer and a twin pak of Pringles.

How much more beer and Pringles can it take? Well, given that giant dress you picked out yourself, we're talking sitdown for two hundred, or at the very least, buffet for one hundred and twenty-five. You've got your work cut out for you. Let's see. Rent a hall, engage a caterer, hire a band, get flowers, find a photographer, order the matchbooks, and hunt up the Jordan almonds. Don't forget the little mints. Your mother wants you to

Others are persecuting you just to ruin your wedding . . .

28

get married pronto because this little old lady she knows who makes these mints and will write your wedding date on them in sugar icing, real tiny, could drop dead any minute.

You had no idea planning a simple wedding would involve so many choices. Are you overwhelmed yet? You should be. And you haven't even begun to make those really hard decisions yet, like whether or not even to serve beer. To you, beer just doesn't seem very, well, wedding-y, but your fiancé begs to differ. Considering that lately you and the groom-to-be have been in a rut, fightwise, these trivial decisions will give the two of you a whole new bickering arena that will no doubt set a tone for pointless arguments in your marriage.

The Parallel Bridal Universe

In the midst of planning this, your major life event, you may become so overwhelmed that when you close your eyes, you see swimming before you a nightmarish collage of midnight-blue lurex cummerbunds, hideous pearlized wedding invitation samples, and dyeable pumps. Well, that's no nightmare. It's a Bridal Expo! Out of a misguided idea that this could help, you've decided to attend one. And what is it? Event planners and local wedding industry merchants team up to sell you the very tackiest nuptials possible. Attend a Bridal Expo and the first thing you'll see, guaranteed, is a woman with hair longer than Crystal Gale's playing the harp. Next, you'll meet the folks from "Mr. Jean-Paul Incorporated," "Harmony House," and "A Touch of Eleganza." These are exactly what they sound like—a bargain-price disc jockey, a

unity candle cottage industry, and a pastel-colored limo service.

Did you ever think you'd make a check out to "Dyeing for you," "Wicks 'n' sticks," or "La Prissy Hen"? You'll see posses of women clamoring to do just this. You'll see mothers and daughters, clad in matching stonewashed ensembles, press-on nails, and frosted hair, fighting in public. "Ma, I sweah to god, our tastes are just too different!" You'll meet "beauty experts" for whom one coat of mascara is too little and twenty-five coats is never enough—yes, makeup addicts in the worst stages of denial. When they are convinced that you finally look gorgeous, you will actually resemble a drunk hooker let loose in the Maybelline factory. Pass them by! Take care not to be cornered by the oddly perky woman who does really bad felt-tip

pen calligraphy. Go, instead, to the caterers' booths, where you won't even be offered samples of the innovative delicacies on their menus—let's face it, we all know what pigs-in-blankets, baked macaroni and cheese, and Swedish meatballs taste like, right?

The bridal fashion show is yet to come—but first they want to warm you up with the sounds of Mario Pasquale and Passione. The band cranks up with a bad cover of "The Rhythm Is Gonna Get You," and for the next forty-five minutes you're treated to top forty hits sung offkey by a balding, mustachioed man in spandex tuxedo pants. Finally, the fashion show begins. It starts, of course, with bridesmaids dresses so choked with ruffles that they'd make your friends look like cir-

cus poodles. Then comes a variety of tuxes, some in a shade that could only be described as K-Mart cobalt. The climax, of course, is the parade of wedding gowns that would leave even Cher feeling cheap. You make a run for the door.

Panting as you fumble in the parking lot for your keys, you'll think your narrow escape from bridal hell is a triumph of the human spirit. Not a chance. They've got your address and phone number. For the next two years you'll be hounded mercilessly. Sometimes they'll tell you you've just won three hundred dollars in a bridal sweepstakes—that is, three hundred dollars off a normally forty-eight-hundred-dollar photography and video package. Other times they'll call to ask you if you'd like your bridal portrait painted—on velvet. Your mailbox will overflow with offers from mortgage companies, cruise lines, car dealers, and yes, even Tupperware, thus reinforcing that sneaking suspicion that your youth is gone forever.

Even if you're embarrassed by bridal magazines and repulsed by bridal expos, you may feel compelled to attend a slightly higher-class affair—the department store bridal event. Now you'll discover—like an old *Twilight Zone* episode—that a strange race of humanoids populate a floor . . . *you never knew existed!*

Elderly women who have committed their lives to telling young folks about fine crystal will be on hand to patronize you. Young men who have no good reason to know what they do about attractive table settings will make you feel like dirt for ever having used torn paper towels as napkins. A string trio playing classical music will have been engaged to make you feel more lowbrow. At the Bridal Event, the importance of choosing all the right flatware, china, appliances, and linens will be stressed, many times over. The pressure is on to register here and now, from women who'd look more like you and me if they didn't have that disapproving set to their tight little lips.

Once trapped there and fed champagne, you'll be dizzily sent on a round robin of sales pitches that you'll actually be quizzed on later, for a few very special prizes. You don't *want* to absorb this information, and yet now you can't help agonizing over which is best for you: T-Fal, Teflon, or Circulon? Can a poly blend dust ruffle hold a pleat *better* than 100 percent cotton? Mattress pads? What for? And just *who are* these people pitching this stuff to you? The same warning sound in your brain that used to sound off in junior high school home ec classes has been shrieking since you walked into this place—but you're not paying attention to it. Something is desperately wrong.

If you listen carefully, beneath the buzz of the crowd, a subliminal message is being played over the sound system. It's saying, over and over, "I love Donna Reed. I want to be like Donna. Donna

Young men who have no good reason to know what they do will make you feel like dirt . . .

is my idol. Donna is good." As you look about, the other brides-to-be seem to have the same glazed-over expressions. Numbly, they fondle flatware, crystal, damask. The fiancés in tow are immune to the Donna chant, and yet powerless to fight it. Except for the rare fussy few you'll overhear hissing in the crystal department—"I don't care what you say. I refuse to serve a highball in an old-fashioned glass"—these men wear a horrified expression that indicates a growing revelation of the shape of things to come.

It seems the night is endless, one demonstration blurring into the next. Your gravyboat knowledge will be put to a searing test. The napkin-folding contest is like a bad dream, your fingers getting thicker and more clumsy by the second. You embarrass yourself badly when you misidentify an angel food cake knife as an Afro comb. Worst of all, you find yourself thinking for the first time in your life that place mats *do* make sense. What has your life come to?

Those test results and the winners are about to be announced. You've endured this so long now, you can't help but be excited. Your head spinning, you imagine a truckload of Waterford, eight hundred place settings of Limoges, anything pricey you could exchange for cash. Okay, okay, at this point

you'd settle for guest towels. The droning continues. They're stringing the crowd along with something critical about . . . what is it? Trivets and coasters!? You begin to wonder if this is actually some twisted right-wing re-education camp designed to whip wayward career women into domestic submission. But finally—finally the winners are announced! No. Not you. A glassy-eyed woman squeals in triumph. Another name—again, not you. Five, six, seven more. Not you. The prizes? Crystal bud vases, porcelain candy dishes, silverplated asparagus tongs. Damn! And you were *that* close.

Get a grip. Since when did you even want napkin rings? Don't worry—come your wedding day, you'll have all these things, in spades.

Would you like to spend a year arguing over hors d'oeuvres with your mother, fighting tooth-and-nail to make your cheapskate father spend an extra seventy-five dollars for a second porta-potty, and discovering a creepy talent for manipulating your fiancé? Of course not. You'd planned on this contest of wills only lasting a few months. But when you begin to make phone calls to find a suitable location for your wedding, you'll find that this decision has already been made for you. When you brightly say, "Uh, June," patronizing wedding directors will lightly sneer, "Of what year, dear?"

It's questions like these that send brides-to-be off the deep end, reinforcing the wedding industry's belief that every woman preparing to get married is so fraught with tension, so wracked with nerves, that she is literally a ticking bomb waiting to go off. Just another sexist generalization? Maybe—or just *maybe* it's drawn from hard-won experience. These veterans of the wedding wars just don't want blood spattered all over their showrooms, that's all. Their policy, in general, is to treat every bride like she is a kind of idiot baby princess, to be alternately coddled and condescended to. You must speak their language in order for them to think that they are speaking yours. Soon you'll find yourself oohing and aahing, cooing and babbling with the best of them. Some of these nuptial nursemaids have been babysitting brides so long that they're literally wedding-happy. Oddly enough, you'll find your mother, the sucker for both weddings and authority figures, going passively along with everything they say. Suddenly your most paranoid ravings have come true. It's you against the world.

Just remember one thing: exactly like the funeral business, the wedding industry is designed to take every possible advantage of you at your most vul-

Their policy is to treat every bride like she is a kind of idiot baby princess . . .

nerable. Being convinced that the Most Beautiful Day of Your Life is entirely your responsibility is enough to send anyone around the bend, and the wedding industry is there to take advantage of this weakness. They'll tell you that forty-five dollars a bottle for Yugoslavian Asti Spumante is a special price, just for you. They'll insist that Cheez Nips and Chex party mix are, at seventy-five dollars per person, the height of elegance. They'll convince you that "The Piña Colada Song" *is* Your Song. The sound of "Daddy's Little Girl" makes them happy. It reminds them that they're making easy money. These people want to pitch you into a deep ravine of bad taste and leave you there. Remember: you walk a fine line between planning the best party ever and organizing a cheesy ritual that will follow you all the days of your life.

All you know is that you want something funky, hip, fun, outside. Your mother wants stately elegance. Even though your wedding vision is still vague, you've been warned that you must find a location soon if you don't want to wed in the twenty-first century. Will you settle on: a disco with no windows but (as the affairs director points out) the biggest mirrored ball in the tristate area? It's little things like this that begin to eradicate your ideal wedding vision. You'll log many miles searching out reception locales, trying to visualize the most beautiful day of your life here, there, and yonder. Then you've got to calculate just how many of your loved ones would travel this far out of their way for you. It's like shopping for real estate. After you begin to see what actually is available, in your price range and on your day, your standards will quickly drop. Eventually, you'll try to get enthused about that nice Elks Hall next to a biker bar and the state's largest landfill that has one open day nine months from now. When you waffle for just a few minutes, you'll find it's been snapped out from under you. Is there no hope for your perfect wedding vision? Read on.

4 THE INCREDIBLE EXPLODING LOVED ONES

Count on one thing:
a year before your wedding,
your mother will already
be worrying about how much
she's going to be worried.

Negotiation or Emotional Blackmail?

Despite learning the ugly truth about the wedding industry, you're still convinced that your wedding will be different. Planning it could still be good, girlish fun—like hosting a doll tea party on a grand scale. And after all, this event is really a day of of deification, worship, and total self-indulgence for you, the bride, right? Unfortunately, others will not see it in exactly the same way. It's times like these that your mother and father may turn from the sweet, loving people who raised you into the kind of parents whose only joy in life is making yours a living hell. If your fiancé at some point impulsively asks them, "But why would you want us to dread coming to our own wedding?" you'll know that things are spinning out of control. Especially if your parents are paying for anything at all. This gives them the funny idea that they can make all the decisions and still say things like "Honey, it's your day. Whatever you want will be fine with us."

Meetings to discuss wedding plans can take on the icy atmosphere of a cold-war summit. You'll bring up the subject of food. Dad will say, "Well, cupcake, what we'll do, see, is just tell everyone on our side to eat before they come. They won't mind, sweetie, and it'll cut back on our expenses"—this in that tone you recognize from the time Daddy went out with the newborn kittens in a bag and came back without them. The topics of alcohol and a band will get the same treatment. "With so many of the older folks going deaf, they wouldn't be able to hear over a band. No one would miss it. And really, who dances anymore?" Elderly relatives who had earlier made generous offers to contribute to the wedding fund—"Whatever it takes, honeybunch, don't you worry about a thing"—become surly when they begin to hear current cost estimates. It seems the last wedding Great Aunt Enid paid for was her son's, in 1952. And of course, your fiancé's creativity only seems to get in the way. His suggestion that your invitations be balloons printed with the slogan SHOW UP OR BLOW UP is met by dour stares. Worse, when he offers to wire up a video "bride-cam" in your headpiece for a strikingly new point of view, your mother will mouth the words "Is this what you really want, honey?" behind her hand.

At this point, you must consider a large, costly traditional wedding very carefully. It could end up costing you or your family as much or more than

the downpayment on a home. But then, you and your parents should ask yourselves this: Will there ever be as special a day as this for you, your family, and friends ever again? Do you want to have memories that will last all your life? And do you (or your mother) have a vindictive need to show a sister/cousin/aunt/best friend just how much better you can do it than they did?

Anyone with the good sense to suggest that the entire event be turned over to a phalanx of professionals will probably be shouted down. How dare they suggest that anyone but you and yours could possibly plan something so personal, so intimate, so completely unmanageable? No professional should ever be made privy to the neurotic logic that motivates your family, and it's definitely not worth explaining. And yet, you will. Again and again. To the florist, the caterer, the baker, and the man behind the counter at the chair rental place. When professionals charge you fifty dollars an hour just for a consultation, you'll want to tell them your family's entire dysfunctional history, so you'll feel like you're getting your money's worth.

You'll want to tell them your family's entire dysfunctional history . . .

Every female you know will offer her opinion. Having planned one wedding in their lives makes them all experts. Even the unmarried have ideas, especially the ones who've been dreaming of this since they were old enough to draw seating charts. Grandmothers, cousins, sisters, sisters-in-law-to-be will all say things like "Sit-down is really so much nicer than buffet. But it's your wedding. Do whatever you want." Of course, if you don't do it their way, well, it won't really *be* a wedding. It'll just be this odd . . . event.

Where others simply insinuate, your mother may have come to the conclusion that this is actually her own wedding. Be patient with her. After all, she's been dreaming about this day ever since they said, "It's a girl." It never dawned on her that you'd have any say. If her own nuptials were not her dream-come-true—because her mother had something to do with it—you are her second chance. And it stands to reason that if she's inviting every single last one of her friends, she may just assume it's her party and not yours. This doesn't bother her in the least. She just figures that you'll get your chance about twenty or thirty years from now, when your daughter gets married.

You may not know it, but ever since you announced your engagement, your mother has been having these little secret meetings with *her*

. . . your mother may have come to the conclusion . . .

friends. They've been whipping each other into an absolute frenzy discussing everything from what she should wear, to what your colors should be, to where she should hold your wedding, to what clothes to buy for Daddy so he won't look like an ape. Many lunches will be consumed as they dig still deeper, to which party supply store is superior and why, to what little wedding favors to have, and to an entire debate about whether people even eat Jordan almonds anymore. The justification for this sneaky organizational orgy? The bridal burden is not yours to carry. Your mother is bending over backward to clear your path down the aisle.

In reality, aside from plotting to get in at the ground floor and run the whole show, these meetings are held to talk your mom into coming back from around the mother-of-the-bride bend so that you won't contract her very contagious prenuptial panic. Unfortunately, the only real effect they have is to turn her into an official wreck, the result of being fed every single wedding disaster story in the world. All you have to do is take one look at her and you'll contract the virus. You aren't her daughter for nothing. A good old mother 'n' daughter bitchfest will ensue. The pitch will go higher and higher, eventually reaching dog-whistle frequency, when suddenly your mother will stop, take one look at you and snap, "I knew you'd be

. . . that this is actually her wedding.

too high-strung to deal with this wedding. I'm going to have to do it all by myself. *I'm just going to have to do everything.*"

If you think you've got a domineering mother, just remember this: Anyone has to be a power freak to raise children. You and I both know that seventeen or eighteen or even thirty years of der Mom Reich is the only thing that kept you from putting an eye out, acting like a wild Indian, or being found dead in a ditch. She can no longer threaten to tan your hide or jerk you baldheaded, but since then, she's found more effective, insidious methods of control. And what event could offer a mother as much opportunity for domination as your wedding?

There's dominating, and then there's an absolute monarchy. Some brides may decide to finish the battle before it's begun and turn the entire campaign over to her Highness, Queen Mom. Case histories abound, but one of the worst was the "Flower Drum Song" wedding assembled by one bright mother, in honor of the Asian groom and his family. Mom got the bright idea to serve Chinese food and dress the bridesmaids in "Suzie Wong"-style dresses. Unfortunately, the husband-to-be was Japanese, and he and his entire clan were offended to see their cultural identity blurred at his own wedding. Worst of all, this mother never really understood why her brilliant planning skills weren't appreciated.

Perhaps it is best to fight for your wedding rights after all—but do it diplomatically. Find a way to work together. Make it clear that you are in control—but include Mom in the decision-making process. In other words, placate her by giving her something simple to do. How could she screw up ordering the flowers, napkins, and tablecloths, as per your exact instructions? Moms are not stupid. She'll know what you're up to, and she won't be treated like a child—so she'll ignore your colors and match everything to her pink dress instead—knowing full well that this is the color you hate most. So, then, it's definitely her wedding. Resist the temptation to invite her to divorce your father and marry your fiancé.

It's stories like these that can make any bride-to-be shiver at the thought of her own mother's potential for matrimonial mayhem. Planning a wedding is never the best time for rational thinking—but guess what? You might not need it. Sometimes, acting like the mature, responsible adult you have become—despite your family's best efforts—can be countereffective to getting the wedding you want. Passive aggression, selective memory, emotional blackmail—all these tools can be your most effective weapons too!

Let the Baby Have Her Way

If trying to get your very traditional family to see you for the responsible career-gal-on-the-go that you really are has never worked before, act in a way that they can more readily relate to. You may get your point across. Having no control is not necessarily the same thing as having no power. You simply have to decide whether or not you want to temporarily give up your identity as a rational being and become the psycho-bride-to-be that everyone knows, fears, and reveres.

Many people are incapable of seeing a rational, assertive woman as anything but a bitch—but in some strange way, they respect a Screaming Harpy.

Regression is the order of the day. Some parents actually see childish bridal behavior as a rite of passage. It may erode all the time and money you've spent to achieve Total Personhood, but, screwy as it may sound, your family may respect you more for it. Becoming She-Ra, Bitch Goddess of Power, may be the only way possible to convince them that you don't want twelve bridesmaids in mauve and ocher, Cesare Nucci's five-piece band playing such timeless party favorites as "The Hokey Pokey," "Alley Cat," and "The Rhythm Is Gonna Get You" and Hawaiian meatballs served as a main course. The only disadvantage of this kind of behavior is that, now that you're finally winning an argument with your family, you may discover you like it. Be warned. After the wedding—as soon as the next morning dawns—they'll get back at you, so make use of your princess rights. You'll never have them again.

TRADITIONAL BRIDE'S
TRADITIONAL WEAKNESSES

- Your family
- His family
- The entire bridal industry
- Your budget
- You

TRADITIONAL BRIDE'S
TRADITIONAL STRENGTHS

You get to:

- make your best girlfriends and sisters-in-law pay through the nose for unflattering dresses they'll never wear again
- make people throw potentially dozens of parties for you

- turn up your nose at their gifts
- refuse to come downstairs for all the parties you've insisted that others throw for you
- throw hissy fits over the tiniest issues
- pout

But wait! there's more! on your wedding day you'll also get to:

- lock yourself into a bathroom
- cry
- refuse to dress until the groom arrives
- make others dress you
- go limp
- swoon at the altar
- have a big scene with your mother/sister/husband in the middle of the reception
- drink too much
- collapse and have to be taken home and put to bed

On your wedding day, lock yourself into a bathroom.

Although your decision to be insane may be temporary, the truly demented in your two families will always choose your wedding as a vehicle for their own particular style of mayhem. Take the mother of the groom who withdrew her support, her showcase home, and her presence for the nuptials at the last minute when she discovered she would not be allowed total control. This forced the event to be shifted, scaled down, and re-scheduled—without her. Would her absence assure a smoother time of it? Not if she collapses on the eve of the wedding and the groom's family members from out-of-town leave the reception early in order to rush to her bedside. True psychosis will always find its own level.

Even if your family is relatively psychologically healthy, there may be some who just can't stand the idea that anyone other than them could be the center of attention. They're easy to spot at your wedding. Just look for the uncle with a neck brace for no real reason, the stepmother with a white dress bigger than yours, or a hyperventilating cousin surrounded by paramedics.

Perhaps your parents are absolutely the opposite of meddling and controlling—nice, polite, repressed people who never raise their voices, carefully try not to impose their ideas, and stay out of the planning process. They may even tell you they're relieved that you're not holding it in their town because they don't have to become involved. Does this mean your wedding will be the perfect, carefree picture you envisioned? Of course not. This is your *family* we're talking about here. Don't be surprised if one day Mom calls up and says, "Honey, I called your aunt to tell her you're not getting married in church," followed by a long silence. What are you supposed to say? She's really informing you of her own deep disappointment. Then she asks if you and the groom are planning to arrive at the wedding site in separate cars. When you say no, she'll insist, in a panic-stricken voice, that you must, because her next-door neighbor Helen doesn't know that you two have been living together for the past three years and if you arrive together in the same car, well . . . somehow, she'll just *know*. And how'll that make her look? Maybe like someone whose own sense of denial has finally been confronted.

If your family has a special talent for incompatibility, this will doubtless put not a small spin on things. You'll be surprised if your divorced parents genially consent to split the wedding costs fifty-fifty—but that'll be the last thing they agree on. After that, phrases like "Oh, that's just so typical," "This is exactly why I left your father,' or "Your mother just has no sense of humor" will abound. Both will demand to see every single last receipt. And so, your wedding plans have become the new arena for yet another round of their old battles.

Stepparents can only add a soupçon of spice to your wedding headaches. There are now dozens of variations on the nuclear family—stepparents, former stepparents, separated step-grandparents, future step-siblings, half-siblings, and perhaps the most piquant of all, the original parents who have not seen one another in twenty-five years. Enough of these scenes, and you can start your own nuclear family holocaust. Aside from some extra-specially careful table seating arrangements, there is no etiquette in the world personal enough to tell you just what to do. You must draw your own figurative or literal DMZ lines and hope for the best. Think positively, but find out if it's possible to rent metal detectors.

Hidden agendas can and will begin to rear their ugly heads from the minute your wedding plans begin. Even the most reasonable mothers can get bent out of shape at the smallest of issues—especially if they're spoiling for a fight. For starters, there's nothing like the old mother-of-the-bride's dress. Etiquette says that the bride's mother (being,

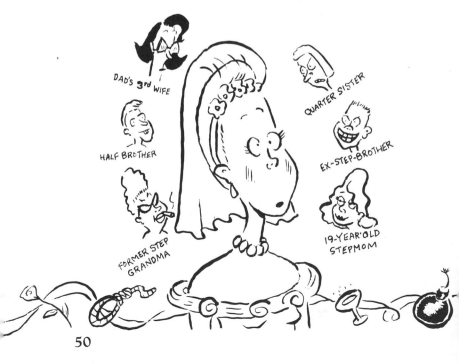

DAD'S 3rd WIFE

HALF BROTHER

FORMER STEP GRANDMA

QUARTER SISTER

EX-STEP-BROTHER

19-YEAR-OLD STEPMOM

theoretically, the second-most important deity at the wedding) gets to pick her dress color and length before the groom's mother gets to choose hers, but don't be surprised if certain maternal noses get pushed out of joint. The etiquette-conscious will be accused of being stuck-up, the non-etiquette-minded branded as savages. Decade-long family feuds have been waged over less.

When his parents and your parents are at war, you and your husband-to-be are the only possible candidates to run interference between the factions. God forbid they actually speak to one another. No, you'll be the one to cushion Mother's rabid disapproval—to your fiancé, who will hopefully soften things even more before negotiating with his dad. This also sets up a fertile little battleground for you and your fiancé about just whose parents are more obnoxious. You'll grit your teeth with frustration when you see the two domineering, overbearing factions acting all kissy-face to each other in a kind of oneupmanship of engagement parties, family barbeques, and luncheons they've insisted on throwing for you. Even though this civility is what you've worked to achieve, part of you would like to see them take it to the mat. If nothing else, this is an early exercise in restraint. After you're married, there'll be plenty more.

What the etiquette books say about family interference is that your wishes should be respected and that everyone should give your their total love and support. You can point this out, but it won't really make any difference to them. This is America. Your fiancé's sister has a god-given right to tell your fiancé not to get you an engagement ring bigger than hers because you're too small-boned to

carry it off—even though you're actually more than a little *zaftig*. Your aunt can say, "I knew your invitations would look like this—you're not going to keep these little pieces of tissue in them, are you?" Your cousin can voice her worry already that you're going to claim names for your future children that she's already reserved. The whole clan is entitled to disapprove of your choice of everything, because, after all, free speech is more important than your feelings.

At this point, you've just got to let some things go—unless you want to start a mental grudge file. And if you're going to do that, well, be ready to take lots of notes so that you'll be sure to remember everything.

REASONS TO GET PUSHED OUT OF SHAPE

Circle the relevant genders and draw arrows between appropriate causes and effects:

CAUSE

- His/your family offers to kick in more money so they can get what they want

- Your/his family think there's nothing wrong with having a good time

- His/your family want a church wedding

EFFECT

- Your/his family think his/your family are being ostentatious and crude

- His/your family think your/his family are acting holier than thou

- Your/his family know that his/your family are going to burn in hell

CAUSE	EFFECT
• His/her family want a big society wedding	• His/your family are just trying to show up your/his family
• Your/his family will pay for liquor if it's going to be some kind of problem	• Your/his family know for a fact that his/your family are nothing but common trash
• His/your mother says if it was up to them they never would have done it that way	• Your/his mother says some people just don't know how to act
• His/your family are offended you aren't having the wedding in their town even though neither of you knows a soul there	• Your/his family are offended that you have chosen a location for the wedding that no one on their side will travel to
• His/your family can't believe that your/his family think that Our Lord Jesus Christ was just another guy	• Your/his family don't know why such a big fuss has to be made over such a minor prophet
• His/your family are completely offended by your choice of department store registry	• Your/his family wonder why you can't register at the K-Mart

It's possible that every last person you're related to will assume that your wedding somehow directly reflects on their taste and their lifestyle. You also run the risk that any member of your family, or your fiancé's family, may see the entire affair as one big conspiracy against them.

All this will become clear when you begin to plan your invitation list. In wedding talk, "Let's keep it small" translates as "Put up your dukes." After all, your parents will want to invite people you haven't seen since you were two years old, their business associates you've never met, and your relatives whom you know only too well. This is their last chance to show off their precious darling in a big frilly dress in public, and if you don't let them there will be hell to pay. Your fiancé's parents will testily insist that they must include every last member of their family. Both sides are just sick that they don't get to invite every last one of their friends. Even though neither his family nor yours wants to pay for a reception for five hundred, it's still somehow your fault. Now, you'd think your fiancé, the man who loves you with all his heart, would cut you some slack—but no. He wants to invite not just his current circle of friends and business acquaintances, but twenty frat broth-

In wedding talk,
"let's keep it small" . . .

ers he hasn't seen in ten years, a woman he lived with before he met you, and a guy he met in a bar last night whose name is "Snots." He'll fight you over officemates you must invite in order to keep your job, your lesbian friend who's still dealing with a big anger thing with men, and your successful ex-boyfriend who makes him feel threatened. As the list gets longer and longer, you'll be calling the caterer and adding more people, trying to see if you can squeeze five more tables into the room and still call what's left over a dance floor, and wonder what American Express means exactly by "no pre-set limit."

Brotherly Love

What better opportunity than a wedding to unearth old unresolved sibling rivalries? You never get too old to want your parents' complete and total love and attention, uninterrupted by those annoying other creatures who happened to populate your house. Even if they do love all their children equally, parents are compelled to focus more on the one who happens to be getting married. Your brothers and sisters won't want to miss the opportunity to regress right along with you.

*. . . translates to
"put up your dukes."*

YOUR BROTHER

- always knew you were Mom and Dad's favorite
- can't believe how stuck up you've gotten
- can't understand what the big deal here is
- thinks your fiancé is a damn sissy twit
- hates you for misbehaving at his wedding when you weren't the center of attention

YOUR SISTER

- always knew Mom and Dad thought you were prettier
- hates that you're getting married first
- hates that you got the good hair
- hates you for not having the wedding both of you planned for Barbie
- knows your parents are definitely, definitely spending more on your wedding than they ever did on hers

They are coming. Don't try to hide, because *They* will find you. *They* will laugh at your pitiful attempts at self-defense. *They* know that modern technology is useless against them. Surrender to . . .

The Incredibly Critical Relatives

They're here. And they're looking for a chink in your armor, a hairline crack, the tiniest flaw in your well-laid wedding plans. There's no point in searching for meaning in the universe when you're related to *The Irrational Ones*. Even if you are the most thoughtful and conscientious person on earth, hypersensitive relations will ferret out minute oversights in your plans—no matter how teensy-weensy—and will accuse you of slighting

them in a deeply personal way. There's no point in defending yourself, or even apologizing. "Oh no. You knew. You *knew* . . ." The sentence invariably trails off. You've got to hand it to them. They're economical. They'll get mileage out of this for years to come, until someone else in your family gets married and your snub gets backlogged in the library of past hurts. Still confused? Here's a case study for the perfectly good, solid reasons relatives come up with for condemning the bride in their midst:

Darlene, a very sensitive, resourceful woman who loves her family, is planning a big wedding to her beloved fiancé, Herman. Her sister Cindy is furious. She can't believe that Darlene would actually plan her wedding in the same year that she's pregnant with her second child, effectively stealing her spotlight. Cindy won't have the baby until three months after Darlene gets married, but Darlene is doing this deliberately because Cindy's pregnant by someone other than her other child's father and everyone knows how judgmental Darlene is. Darlene's other sister, Cherie, isn't speaking to her because Darlene didn't ask her to be a member of the wedding. Cherie has a closet full of bridesmaid's dresses that she's always bitching about, and she and Darlene aren't that close since, in junior high school, Darlene gave Cherie a Pez and told her it was acid and she freaked out anyway and went and told the school nurse she was on LSD and got in big trouble. Cherie says Darlene should've made the gesture. Darlene did ask Cherie if she wanted to "help out" with things, but why should she help out if she doesn't even get to be a member of the wedding? That's another thing. Darlene *didn't* ask her cousin Suzanne to help, and

everyone knows Suzanne loves weddings. Since she lost her job after her married boss she was having the affair with was charged with fraud and came this close to taking Suzanne down with him, she could use something to get her mind off that awful depression she's been in.

Darlene's mom is mad at her because her Aunt Evelyn is a very good seamstress and would have been thrilled to make the wedding dress but did Darlene even discuss it with her? No, she just went right out and bought a dress *without consulting anyone*! Aunt Evelyn's feelings are really really hurt and of course she blames Darlene's mom for not

raising her right in the first place, and Darlene's mom has to listen to her fuss anyway even though she knows that the reason Darlene didn't ask Aunt Evelyn to sew it for her is because you can consult 'til you're blue but Aunt Evelyn makes things *her* way and more likely than not with rickrack, but still, Darlene should've called Evelyn. Of course, Uncle Desmond is mad too, but he's not talking about it, because he never talks about it, never talks about anything, but he's sick and tired of his brother Willis not being sent an invitation and being completely forgotten about by the women in this family. Willis still lives somewhere in Canada, Calgary, or something, where Desmond is from, and it's not like he'd really come, because Willis doesn't like to leave the house the week his pension check is due, but Desmond just doesn't like Willis being left out.

Grandma has a frosty tone in her voice when she speaks to Darlene on the phone these days because Darlene didn't think it was important

enough to send the invitations to the family back in North Carolina until just two weeks ago, and they arrived too late for them to make plans, and even though they practically never leave their own trailer, much less the state, they ought to be treated just like anyone else. Darlene asked did they mind, seeing as everyone knows they don't ever go anywhere, and no, they didn't seem to, but Grandma did. Another thing is, when Great Aunt Ruthie drove two hours, and at her age, just for Darlene's shower, Darlene didn't rush over and give her a big kiss right away when she got out of her car. It doesn't matter that Darlene saw her three weeks ago at Uncle Honey and Aunt Inez's fiftieth wedding anniversary. She should've kissed her right then and not waited for her to come up the walk. Great Aunt Ruthie isn't surprised by Darlene's behavior—not since she found out Darlene's not getting married in her own people's church, by her own people's minister, but in some church no one ever heard of except maybe the groom's people, who're from some county you never even heard listed in the snow watch on the TV weather report. In fact, Darlene might have just made it up to disguise that they're not from anywhere you'd even like to think about.

And then, of course, there's Darlene's fiancé Herman Foster's family. Herman's sisters are calling her "that woman," and Herman's mother, Mrs. Foster, has spent the last week crying her eyes out over . . .

Needless to say, the song of the *Incredibly Critical Relatives* could easily go on and on and on. But by now, you doubtless know all the words. But perhaps your family isn't like this. Maybe they're all generous, rational-minded folks who like to think they know the *real* you. People who know you better than you know yourself can be so annoying. They analyze your moods, monitor your every gesture, and look at you when they think you're not looking. Because they anticipate it, your clan may read hysteria into your normal everyday behavior. They'll catch you in the most commonplace acts— like brushing your hair—and say things like, "You know, I don't think you're really ready to get married." Right about now, it dawns on you that the whole point of this wedding ordeal is that it will make you glad to leave your family and cleave unto your husband.

5 THE RULES OF ENGAGEMENT

Meeting the Opposition on the Bridal Battlefield

IT WILL TAKE WEEKS, and probably months, to search out services appropriate, affordable, and available for your wedding. Just what is it about good taste that costs so much more than bad taste? How can asparagus spears be more expensive than Hawaiian meatballs? Why would the lawn of an old mansion cost three times more than a catering hall with flocked wallpaper, a crystal chandelier, and a sweeping staircase? It's as though everyone in the wedding industry has a secret price guide to penalize anyone with any style. They do.

Invitation to Disaster

Maybe you'd like something that stands out, something a little different from your basic copperplate engraved wedding invitation. These days, thanks to the burgeoning wedding invitation catalog business, a couple has literally hundreds of choices of invitation styles to choose from. Most of them involve pearlized, embossed calla lillies, die-cut brides and grooms, gold foil accents, and lugubrious mottoes like "Precious Moments." At the touch of an 800 number, operators are standing by to encourage you to order wedding invitations that have been reworded to sound more warm and cuddly:

> Our love is the flower that blossoms
> Our joy . . . its lasting perfume
> We invite you to witness with us
> a miracle of love
> that fills the sky with timeless love
> On Saturday, August first
> Nineteen hundred and ninety-two
> at six o'clock
> St. Patrick's Church
> 193 Maple Drive
> Hardyville, Illinois

Not only are you invited to something that sounds suspiciously like a sixties-style encounter group, but on the outside of the invitation is often the kind of poem that would embarrass even Rod McKuen:

> Celebrate with us
> as we join together . . .
> Like the flames
> of two candles
> that unite
> to form a single flame,
> we will shine
> with greater brightness
> and strength—
> yet suffer none
> in our individuality.

Just in case none of this is personal enough for you, these mail-order printers invite you to write your *own* poetry:

First of all we are friends
  We have been from the start
Our fondness took us by surprise
  So softly in our hearts
The feeling grew too big for us
  As we began to care
So today we pledge a love
  That we want you to share
A day of happiness and joy
  As we commit our lives
A dreamy girl, a bashful boy
  Becoming man and wife

Even if you're not a poet, keep in mind that any kind of improvisation is bound to set a tone. For example, "Vic and Shoshana welcome you to witness, on this day, the melding and intertwining of their souls" hints that your wedding ceremony will definitely involve the mentioning of rainbows and sunsets, that your caterer will rely heavily on bran, and that your guests will be forced to dance to New Age music. Worse still, these kind of invitations could influence your guests in their choice of wedding gifts. A magic healing crystal might seem to them more appropriate than Waterford. Unless this appeals to you, perhaps you should stick to the slightly silly but traditional sound of just requesting the pleasure of their company. And this way, maybe people really will show up.

Catering to Your Whims

There are people in the wedding industry whose entire base of power is built around convincing you that planning your nuptials has robbed you of the ability to make informed, adult decisions. When the fabulous, famous caterer who has done you the enormous favor of squeezing you in says, "Well, of course, I'm open to all your suggestions, but I *really* just want everything to go *my* way, heh, heh," you chuckle at his wry, clever wit. But then when he keeps overriding all your ideas and saying to your fiancé, Robert, "Oh, now, Bobby, I don't think we'd better let her do that, do you?" it's hard to maintain your sense of humor. If you try to object to this treatment, he'll respond with a "Honey, you're just a nervous wreck already!" If you say you're not, he'll counter with, "Of course you are. *All* brides are nervous wrecks." To add insult to injury, he'll tell you, in a whisper loud enough for your fiancé to hear, that "It's a shame your gorgeous Bobby is going to waste—he's *such* a golden boy!" The only way you're going to get what you want in this situation is to use Robert as leverage. Promise the caterer a certain amount of time alone with Bobby *if* he'll do the peapods en papillote, the pâté en croûte, *and* the huîtres provençale. Naturally, you'll feel some qualms about using the man you love as a mere instrument of your whims—but he can take care of himself, and this is your wedding day we're talking about here. Who said you couldn't make informed, adult decisions?

Let Them Eat Cake

Of course you'll want to pay special attention to choosing your wedding cake—the second most sacred object at your wedding, next to your dress. This makes sense, since they're both the same basic shape and color. Visit every bakery in town. Insist that your maid-of-honor come along and be your official taster. It's her duty to gain weight for you.

These days, wedding cakes come in every conceivable shape, color, flavor, and size, unless, of course, your caterer makes the cake part of his package deal, in which case, you could end up with something that looks like it's been sitting in the window of a bakery for the past five years and tastes like a tall Twinkie. Hopefully, though, your cake can be a deeply personal statement, as lavish or as simple as you like. All bakers want to talk you into ordering Versailles in cake form. Some will even try to talk you into having an actual fountain between tiers, with water colored to match your theme. This can be a dramatic effect, pleasing to the eye, unless, of course, you've chosen yellow. If you insist, despite objections from your baker, on the ultra-simplicity of a sheet cake, he will get back at you by decorating it with only the groom's and your names with that tacky Close-up toothpaste-type frosting, in the tiniest lettering imaginable.

Of course you'll want to pay special attention to choosing your wedding cake . . .

No wedding cake is complete without at least three or four little girls to linger longingly around your cake during your reception, but remember—most bakeries will not provide them, so do invite some.

When Bad Things Happen to Good Cakes

A wedding cake at a wedding is like a meringue pie at a clown convention. Something is just begging to happen to them. Tents fall on them, mirthmakers cha-cha right into them, they topple of their own free will—these things happen. This is not the end of the world. Here's a secret—nobody, except those little girls, is that crazy about cake to start with, and your guests are dying to see something—anything—go wrong. You've satisfied their needs by providing some much-needed drama.

The Photographer

I know what you wanted. You wanted that photographer who took those incredibly classy black-and-white candid shots of all the Kennedy kids' weddings, so that your wedding, and your life, in retrospect, would look like you actually lived in that rarified atmosphere of American royalty. Well, he's not available, but hundreds of other photographers are. Of course, they'll all want to talk you into pictures more embarrassing than your high school senior photo—you know, where they forced you to look winsomely over your shoulder, into the camera? They'll wangle about phrases like "misties,"

"montages," and "romantics." They'll suggest cutesy poses, like re-creating the marriage proposal—only in a more ideal fashion, where your fiancé actually does get down on bended knee and you sit there looking like a princess, only in sportswear. Or how about the two of you hand-in-hand on a cliff overlooking the setting sun? That sounds to you like a very picturesque documenting of a suicide pact. Worst of all, and so frightening you don't even want to think about it—how about the two of you standing in front of your mother's drapes? Auuuuggggh! Remember: wedding photographers are in league with the devil, or at least those people who plan bridal expos.

Florists

"No baby's breath!" You can scream it till you turn into a dyed-blue daisy—but the florist will blithely ignore you. Baby's breath is the Hamburger Helper of the floral world—ballast that ostensibly makes less look like more. You might've gone in clutching pictures of arrangements with peonies, dahlias, and cabbage roses as big as your head, but after about

They'll suggest cutesy poses . . .

two seconds of cost estimating, you'll have to scale down your dream just a tad—to two irises, one stalk of freesia, and a fern sprig "filled out" with baby's breath in a sprayed-silver basket. What about your bouquet? Well . . . do you like carnations?

Music to Your Ears

Of course, you've got to have music for your ceremony—and of course it's got to be live music, played by real musicians. To have someone fumbling with a casette and a boom box is tad too reminiscent of a wedding chapel in Reno. Now you've got to decide what to play and who to have play it. Will it be, after all, Rapunzel the harpist playing Pachelbel's Canon in D (that classical thing everyone knows as the "G.E. Soft Light Bulb Song") a thin-voiced singer doing a really, really sincere version of Paul Stookey's "The Wedding Song," or the wedding band pianist, who looks like Marty Allen's twin, doubling at the ceremony? (He's been in lounge-act land so long he'll put an appropriate, cocktailish flourish on the end of Mendelssohn's "Wedding March.") Again, there are alternatives. You don't have to be one of the billions and billions of brides served by "Sunrise, Sunset" or "We've Only Just Begun." Use your imagination. Choose something of deep personal meaning to you and your beloved. Your fiancé's roommate's speed-metal trio could play an up-tempo version of Billy Idol's "White Wedding," with a ten-minute guitar solo. Your avant-garde musician friend could perform an original piece based on atonal chord structures. Or, when was the last time you heard "Here Comes the Bride" played on the musical saw? These ideas suggest an

element of fun in an otherwise ho-hum ceremony.

Don't forget the music for the reception. Your friends and fiancé will scream for reggae, rap, afro-pop—but somehow, mysteriously, just as you wound up with that big white dress, you'll probably wind up with a wedding band. Bands who play exclusively for weddings are very democratic—they know they can't please everyone, so they usually don't please anyone, except maybe your great aunt. They'll play songs you've heard only in elevators, like "Paper Roses," but they always give a tip o' the hat to top-forty tunes. It's always a treat to hear a middle-aged Italian man sing "Billie Jean."

Many brides, if the parents haven't put a stranglehold on such decisions, will leave the band choice up to the groom. This is a bone you can throw him so he doesn't bitch about the tiny food, the monkey suit, and that no-beer decision. It also gives him the chance to go out at night to do band "research" and stay away from what he's started calling the House of Wedding Horror. One groom we know engaged a hot little blues quartet, only to be awoken at 7:00 A.M. on his wedding day to be told the band was stranded a thousand miles away with a broken-down truck. He knew if he didn't come through, his bridegroom ass was grass. Luckily he remembered a good place—the only place—to recruit a band on Saturday at 11:20 A.M. was the city park. Just as luckily, the guests all thought a group that did Beatles songs—all in

Spanish—was fun and different. And of course, there's a certain panache to having a drummer with no teeth.

Maybe you had this idea that that society combo you engaged that performed at Reagan's birthday party will have that big band sound everyone loves to dance to—but what does Reagan know? He wears a hearing aid. Keep in mind you can always dub onto your wedding video the music you had in mind in the first place, thus giving the impression that Nelson Riddle came back from the dead just to play your reception.

Now that you've made your choices, you can start to worry. Even though you've been reassured that the caterer does do things in a nouvelle way, it doesn't help when they ask questions like "Do you want the mashed potatoes dyed blue?" This isn't doing a thing to dispel your growing paranoia that they all really do want to send you over the edge into that chasm of cheesiness. On top of it all, if your mother has anything at all to do with these plans, often, they'll go over your head and call her to see what *she* really wants. Why, why, why won't they allow you to do what you've always dreamed of—to forge your reputation as a tasteful trendsetter and bon vivant? Perhaps you've forgotten something here: *You have no control.*

The Cocktail Hour

Recently, people have felt compelled to find imaginative ways to entertain guests during that nebulous time after the ceremony and before the reception cranks up. Someone thought that everyone would get a sentimental thrill from seeing slides of the bride and groom from childhood until the present day. Now, think about it. Isn't it enough that they bought gifts and the appropriate clothing, set the time aside, and traveled here to be with you on your special day? Don't take it personally, but most of your friends and family would rather be shot in the head than look at pictures of you and your friend Skeeter at the sophomore car wash or your new husband on the toilet as a toddler. Don't even *think* about magicians or mimes, either. People are not so hard to please. In these days of abstinence, fitness, and safe sex, a simple cocktail hour—drinks and hors d'oeuvres—have become to adults what cupcakes and punch are to kindergarteners: an indescribable thrill.

Keeping Your Guests Entertained

Remember, this may be the most beautiful day of your life, but for your guests, it's just another party—but with a twist. As much as your more sincere friends believe that they want to be with you on this special day, a small voice in the back of their minds is saying, "Maybe the cake will fall over!" or "Maybe someone will get pushed in the pool!" Of course, the secret favorite of all is that someone will stand up and say, "Stop the wedding!" Don't get me wrong. I'm sure all your guests wish you the very best, but every red-blooded American has an underlying thrill-seeking desire to see things go wrong—especially at hyperorchestrated events. Of course, you hope to disappoint these baser urges, but you *can* titillate your guests by keeping them guessing. Have the band play songs like "One's on the Way," "Papa Don't Preach," or "You're Having My Baby." Greet

veiled comments from your more suspicious guests with a blank stare. Nine months from now you can savor their disappointment.

Weddings Across America

America is a country rich in diverse wedding traditions. It's wonderful that regional customs have not yet become homogenized, but it's also another problem to face if you're marrying someone who comes from another part of the country. Weddings are like family holidays: we all assume that everyone else has Christmas the same way, and when we discover that other families have different traditions, our most natural impulse is to assume that they are . . . well, mentally ill. After all, anything different from what you're used to is just deviant behavior, right? On top of all this, there are enormously varying definitions of the word *small*, just as different families have widely divergent interpretations of what *loud* is. When dealing with your in-laws and their expectations about your wedding, it helps to have this brief guide, so that you can start to sort out what are old, regional customs and what are simply your in-laws' twisted minds.

SOUTHERN WEDDINGS

The typical southern Protestant wedding has certain time-honored traditions and codes that are never altered. Not for our devout southern cousins are out-of-control hedonistic hymeneals. Pleasure-seeking sybarites should think twice about applying for marriage licenses below the Mason-Dixon line, because there, unless you come from old money, weddings have nothing to do with fun.

73

From the creepy ceremony by the salesman-for-Jesus minister to the nonalcoholic reception with a bunch of people who won't talk to each other, to the throwing of the silk (tacky) flower bouquet, you can clock in at (thank god) under an hour. And this is after getting ten or twelve bridesmaids, groomsmen, ushers, and a ringbearer and flower girl to go to the trouble of dressing up in matching outfits for you. Your reception is always held in the church basement or a Sunday School room. Never fancied-up for the occasion, they figure that being surrounded by pictures of Jesus at your reception is ironic reminder enough about that evil thing you'll be doing later tonight. Your second-string girlfriends, not quite good enough to have been bridesmaids, are recruited to do the serving, clad in little frilly aprons that match your colors. Now, your best second-string girlfriend serves the cake. Your second-best second-string gal pal pours that lime-sherbet punch. Two more of your second-stringers will stand there looking helpless in their aprons, since it's really not possible to do anything more than let people know they may help

themselves to the peanuts and mints. What about food? That *is* the food, that's all you get, and no one ever sits down to eat it. Mingling is forbidden. You just stand there, eat your cake, sip your punch, and leave. Soon you'll be on your way to Gatlinburg, Tennessee, to play Hillbilly Goofy Golf, walk hand-in-hand down the main drag, and watch tube socks being made on machines in the windows of souvenir shops.

Not all southerners refuse to bar fun at weddings. Indeed, the most opulent weddings in the country are held by southern high society—in the biggest way possible. An exclusive country club is the usual reception locale—unless of course, it can't accommodate, oh, say, a thousand guests. No, if a location large enough can't be found, Daddy will just snap up a hotel and renovate it, or buy a few acres of valuable riverfront property and landscape it—just for his precious Sugar's big day. You can bet at weddings like these there's going to be more than peanuts and mints. It's customary to impress everyone with the most elaborate tableaus of flown-in, out-of-season shellfish,

caviar, and, of course, champagne. At an event already excessive by any standards, drinking yourself into a stupor is de rigueur. Someone's got to make up for the Baptists.

Southern white trash* is like a compromise between Uppity Baptist and those rich show-offs. How is this possible? Well, you get married in the church, you have your cake-and-punch reception in the Sunday School, but you sneak your beer in the church parking lot. Drinking in close proximity to automobiles sets everyone at ease enough to reconvene at the bride's parents', where guests pick their way past assorted car parts and four or five big muddy yard dogs to squeeze into the mobile home unit and watch the newlyweds open special gifts like matching I'M WITH HIM/HER BECAUSE HE/SHE DESERVES THE FINEST T-shirts—from the parents of the groom. Bring your own malt liquor is the policy, but that doesn't mean the end of southern hospitality. Cold Duck is served the crowd of thirty—one bottle, anyway. The fun doesn't stop. If you hang around long enough, you can follow the happy couple home and help them put their new waterbed together.

THE MIDWESTERN WEDDING

There's nothing like a midwestern, middle-class wedding for sheer practicality. Far from being fashionably late, you'll find that many of your guests—especially the legions of little old ladies who live for these events—will actually arrive early to get good seats in church. People will race to get to the

*Keep in mind that these wedding customs are not limited to the South, but are nationwide—wherever white trash is found.

reception—usually held at places like the Croatian Crest Club, the Abdullah Shrine Temple, or a big old Knights of Columbus hall—eager to be first in line for the chow. The chow is always a buffet, consisting of sliced ham and cheese, roast beef, snowflake rolls, potato salad, and cole slaw. This is unless, of course, the mother-of-the-bride's pride is at stake. Then she will have had to slave over a hot stove for the last six months,* in which case there may be a stunning array of freshly defrosted casserole dishes and finger foods. Those same elderly ladies who took all the good seats supervise the serving and make sure no one hogs. For some reason, they refer to a wedding reception with dancing as a combination wedding party *and* dance. There's an art to finding a band that can play straight-ahead rock 'n' roll and those crowd-pleading polkas. Not as straight-laced as their southern cousins, midwesterners—even the Methodists—will tolerate liquor at a wedding reception. This may consist of a full bar, open for only as many minutes as the father of the bride can afford—but generally runs toward kegs of beer. Midway through what are usually marathon-length receptions, the men get together and steal the bride, and sometimes the women abduct the groom. This is called a Shivaree. The kidnappers don't really know what they're supposed to do with the newlyweds except maybe drive them around for a while and stop for a couple of drinks. Generally they're relieved when the bride suggests that maybe it's getting time to go back and cut the sheet cake. There is a wedding cake as well, but

*Not to mention sewing your wedding gown, her mother-of-the-bride dress, your maid-of-honor's dress, and all the bridesmaids' dresses as well.

that's just for looks. That's right. These people *Have* their cake and eat it too. What could be more practical? The dollar dance, of course, a big tradition in America's heartland, which might make it possible for the bride and groom to go to Disneyworld instead of just drive to the Ozarks, buy matching WE'RE ON OUR HONEYMOON T-shirts, take in a giant water slide or two, and come home again.

THE MAFIA PRINCESS WEDDING

From blue-collar families taking out second mortgages to pay for them, to Cosa Nostra chieftains pulling out all the stops, package wedding receptions are an institution across the northeastern United States. The institution you're committing yourself to usually looks like the fantasy of a thirteen-year-old girl from Staten Island-Mediterranean-cum-Tudor-cum-Vegas, with swans. Your basic low-end princess wedding is programmed down to the last detail. At the reception hall, every member of the wedding and their family are announced as they enter. This way great aunts in their thirty-year old blond mink stoles and great uncles in their best plaid dinner jackets become lords 'n' ladies in a kind of cheesy faux-Louis XIV court fantasy. Aggressive video crews aim cameras

at the guests' tonsils as they messily carbo-load on baked ziti and veal parmesan. The wedding director has the jolly manner of a Catskills nightclub emcee, combined with an uncomfortable undercurrent of menace. Employing this, he orchestrates the event to a fare-thee-well, commanding the bride to dance with her father to "Daddy's Little Girl," the groom to dance with his mother to "Memories," and offering a play-by-play as the bride and groom do the dollar dance with every single guest. The band, with a Tony Bennett impersonator, plays everything from "Danny Boy" to "Dirty Dancing." Every time the guests tap their glasses with their silverware, the bride and groom must kiss, insuring, after only a few times, an ingrained Pavlovian response to one another. People accustomed to attending these events are scandalized if the same exact chain of events—say, the Venetian dessert table is not laid simultaneously with the liqueur course—is not followed to the letter.

The cost of this event is offset by the social pressure applied for your guests to be very generous. No gifts are brought to the reception. The bride has already raked it in big time at countless showers in which a typical gift is a washer and dryer, or a thirty-foot boat. Instead, at the end, everyone lines up in a receiving line to present the

bride and groom with envelopes—a minimum of one hundred dollars, please.

If you have a problem with decision-making, this is the wedding for you. The only choices you'll be offered are whether or not you want the mashed potatoes dyed to match your theme and whether you want the chopped liver sculpted into a horsehead or a bust of your late father.

THE CALIFORNIA WEDDING

In California, there's nothing so touching as a hippie mom giving away her hippie/punk/surfer son in a ceremony on the beach presided over, as usual, by a Unitarian minister/chiropractor/screenwriter. But don't use this as a guideline. Remember: if you're going to have a hippie wedding, it's inappropriate to plan it at all. But I don't want to play mind games with you, because I know you're looking for, like, a wedding guru here. Trippy attire for the mother of the bride is torn (blue) jeans, a halter top, thongs, hoop earrings, and a cigarette. No one will be bummed if the bride's dad wears what he always does, a Grateful Dead T-shirt and day-glo jammers. More important, though, is that you use your imagination. It's your thing. Do what you wanna do. You want more? God, you've got such a *western* mind. Okay, the groom always looks bitchen with a half-shaven head and a dashiki. And the bride should definitely wear, okay, like a vintage black velvet evening dress with a black lace shawl, and lots of silver skull jewelry. Think of Stevie Nicks. If your guests arrive looking like they thought they were going to a normal wedding, freak them out. Seating them on the ground next to the amp while the groom's speed-metal band

plays "Dude Looks Like a Lady" will blow their minds. Go with the flow, and if you can't do that, after the ceremony, turn to the only person there wearing heels and pearls and ask him what comes next.

Kids, Don't Try This at Home

What? After all that, you just want to keep it simple? Well, they say there's nothing like a wedding at home for intimacy, comfort, and relaxed charm. That's what they say, but if you look up *home wedding* in the dictionary, the definition is "major home improvement." Your mother suddenly realizes that her home cannot possibly be opened to dozens or possibly hundreds of guests without being transformed into the showcase she always knew it could be. After all, it's only a matter of taking out a wall here, re-doing a kitchen there, repairing major termite damage while they're at it, and that roof has just got to be . . . Trying to make wedding plans with a woman who is living without a bathroom can really be a drag. A nice luncheon out while out shopping with Mom can turn into a tirade about loan officers, irresponsible contractors, drunk carpenters, erratic electricians, and drywall. Do you, precious bride, need to hear this? Perhaps now you'll know that "home wedding" always means someone else's home, somewhere else, some other time.

Wedding Datebook Chart

SIX TO TEN MONTHS BEFORE

- act all happy for a week
- run up a huge phone bill telling everyone

- fight about the engagement ring—he casually suggests that it's a silly, unnecessary anachronism—you correct this thinking
- have a fight about how many of his friends can come
- argue about where to have the wedding
- put off thinking about paying for it, hoping that parents will
- plan to invite just close friends and family—about thirty people
- laugh about how absurd and pretentious bridal magazines are

THREE TO SIX MONTHS BEFORE
- have a fight about your choice of maid of honor
- with your parents, avoid the subject of just exactly who is paying and how much will be spent
- fight with your mother about her guest list of "family friends" you haven't seen since you were three
- secretly buy twelve bridal magazines. Be amazed at all the wedding etiquette you never knew about. Hope other people do.
- agree to expand guest list to "sixty, tops"
- fight with mother over wedding dress style

TWO TO THREE MONTHS BEFORE
- still avoid specifics on who's paying for what
- alienate your sister-in-law by demanding that she throw you a shower
- fight with your fiancé about inviting business associates
- discover that sixty invitations means one hundred and twenty because nobody goes to a wedding alone

- fight with seamstress over wedding dress fitting

ONE MONTH BEFORE

- alienate your siblings by requesting they "behave" at the wedding in front of your new in-laws
- be disgusted at how nobody RSVP's or even seems to care about proper etiquette anymore
- fight with your future mother-in-law about her guest list
- expand guest list to one hundred and sixty-five because many have sent in their response cards with the notation "plus 8"
- fight with your mother over the wording of the invitation
- fight with your fiancé over invitation design
- fight with the clergyman over the wording of the ceremony

ONE WEEK BEFORE

- alienate out-of-town friends who wanted to bring their kids
- call those who haven't RSVPed to find out if they're coming; try to discourage them from coming
- have a huge fight with your fiancé about the basis of your entire relationship, which turns out to be based on your fiancé's fear of death, which he's never mentioned before
- worry about everything

THE DAY BEFORE

- notice that your face has broken out
- start wondering how you can avoid holidays with both families

- grimace when your fiancé asks if it's too late to invite more people now

ON THE WEDDING DAY

- step onto the emotional rollercoaster with your mother by your side as you get dressed and put on your makeup
- tear up and enjoy the blur that passes before your eyes
- be surprised afterward when Mom and Dad, with their new nineties-type attitude, announce that they're allowing you to pay for your own wedding and ask to be reimbursed for all their deposits before you leave for your honeymoon.

6 SHOWER ME!

*Ask not what you can do
for others. Ask what others
can do for you.*

IS YOUR NEED FOR POTPOURRI, boudoir pillows, and lingerie really so great that you'd risk blackmailing your friends into spending time and money planning a shower for you? *Of course* it is. Now is the time for you to go into bridal training by making sure that you're the center of attention as often as possible. Build to the stunning crescendo that is Your Wedding by forcing your by-now resentful maid of honor, next-to-best friends, relatives, and officemates to throw not just one but dozens of parties for you. I know someone who had a lingerie shower, a miscellaneous shower, a coffee, a cookout, a rice-bag party, an informal tea, and a rehearsal dinner. I was impressed until informed that the same eleven people attended every event. Unless you live in a small southern town, don't get your hopes up too high for this sort of excess. If you're lucky, though, your wedding shower will include a bridal bingo, candy underwear, and an Asti Spumante headache. Someone will have broadcast the idea, wrongly, that you just adore anything with ducks on it. Never mind. The real purpose behind a shower is to allow you to adjust gradually to being the center of the universe.

There's a dark secret behind all showers, teas, luncheons, and weddings held in the homes of relatives or friends of relatives. These events are not thrown in your honor—no. They are not prepared as an expression of the love felt for you and the man you have chosen as your life's mate. No, these receptions are assembled so that one woman can stand behind her sterling tea service at the end of the buffet table and say, "Cream? One lump, or two?" You may find that here is competition among mothers, mothers-in-laws, aunts, cousins, and family friends to finally have the opportunity to haul out of their original packages the fifty-gallon coffee urns, the aspic trays, and the shrimp forks that *they* got as presents at *their* weddings. There is always the danger that they'll engage in ugly tong wars.

Since your role as a bride-to-be has grown larger-than-life, don't be surprised that these kinds of showers rarely have anything to do with you. It's for your mother. Just being the mother of the bride is like being the mother of a celebrity—or, if she plays it to the hilt, like being the Blessed Mother. Credit, after all, is taken for having produced something so sacred as a bride. Your mom has waited all your life for this moment, and this is her last chance to show you off in a proprietary way. It's the least you can do to curtsey, twirl in your nice party dress, and allow the ladies to painfully pinch your cheek one last time. There is another truth about these functions. All these old ladies who haven't seen you in twenty years now have the chance to judge whether or not you have been raised correctly. The test will consist of questions like these:

- Can you enthuse about a grocery coupon organizer?
- Can you identify correctly the item that came with your potholders as a matching apron—for your detergent bottle to wear?
- Can you listen sympathetically to an elderly woman's quavery-yet-detailed description of her recent hysterectomy?
- Can you pronounce a mayonnaise-jello salad "pure heaven" *and* beg for the recipe?

One bride I know had an ideal shower. Her mother's bridge-club friends, shower-happy souls that they were, wanted to have one for her, but the bride lived many hours away and was much too busy to come home just for an afternoon. The ladies threw it for her in absentia. They played shower games, they ate shrimp wiggle, they had a middle-aged ball. Her mother got to play surrogate bride, open all her presents, and act far more genuinely enthused than her daughter ever possibly

"Cream? One lump or two?"

could have. It was the almost perfect solution. Almost. The bride still had to write all the thank-you notes.

There are showers, and then there are *showers*. In these liberated times, setting the tone depends on whether or not older female family members are present. Mixing girlfriends and female relatives can be awkward. The almost obligatory male strip-per at the shower pales before more creative, devil-ish acts—such as creating a board game tailormade with agonizing trivia questions about the sexual history of the guest of honor. There are just some things a mother doesn't want to know. Your taste in undergarments may be one of those questionable areas. Though a lingerie shower doesn't sound right off like an inappropriate place for Mom, think about it. After opening that nice high-necked flannel nightgown Mom got from Lanz, it's going to be difficult for you and your friends to squeal over the lamé bustier, the push-up bra, and the Hot Stuff Warming Massage Oil. Even if you do have, say, a thoroughly modern grandmother, you may feel uncomfortable about getting edible underwear from her.

The shower thrown for you by your officemates can introduce more anxiety-ridden elements. For one thing, the girls at work really do resent shell-ing out month after month, year after year, for shower gifts for someone they make small talk with twice a day in the hallway. The office shower is what the potpourri industry depends on. You may note a pattern in the gifts you receive. More than seven or eight of a particular item at any one shower—say, like sachet-scented clothes hangers—and it's easy to figure out that news of a sale spread like wildfire among the unimaginative. Sometimes

even your friends can surprise you. Boy, you think you know people, you think you trust them, and then they go and give you *placemats*. Don't they know that this is the adult equivalent of getting new socks and undershirts for Christmas? Calm down. Shower Ennui has set in. You may not believe me, but someday you'll catch yourself gift-wrapping potpourri-scented oven mitts and you'll be a little more sympathetic. Try to forgive—except in the case of the truly unforgivable, and that is the gift of *one* towel, *one* guest towel, and *one* washcloth. None of these match or coordinate with any other towel you'll ever own, and they will haunt your linen closet for years.

The most annoying part of these showers is that, now that your workmates have forked over $8.53 for things like coasters with cats on them, they expect to be invited to your wedding. You'd been hoping to avoid just this. It can take some pretty bald-faced lying ("What? Exactly when did postage go up again?") and hiding behind boxes of xerox toner to get around this.

But maybe you think you're not the shower type. And neither are your friends. Maybe you think your little crowd of smarty-pants college buddies are all just too discerning, erudite, and accomplished to take part in something this silly. Maybe you think you're all just going to get together for a quiet, dignified dinner somewhere. (Nobody's even mentioned that S-word.) Don't make the worst mistake of your life. Missing out on a real shower would be like getting a total anesthetic for childbirth. This is something you simply must experience to be a Total Woman.

Make your friends change that reservation from that elegant little bistro to the silliest Caribbean/

Tahitian/Mexican restaurant in town. White wine? Bite your tongue! Sugary tropical drinks with names like "Sex on the Beach" are the catalyst needed to make you all act like the girls you really are. It's your brainy buddies' absolute duty to make sure that the level of intelligent conversation decays as rapidly as possible. A few suggestions:

- debate bikini wax vs. electrolysis
- decide who's got a cuter butt, Mel Gibson or Bruce Springsteen
- admit which stupid top-forty songs you secretly thrill to
- discuss why female tennis stars are always so ugly
- justify your weight by saying that, if you were a famous actress or top model and paid to look good, dieting would be more important to you; then order another pu-pu platter

This is a shower, for heaven's sake, not a seminar. Even though men will go on regressing for years, this may be your last shot at utterly gushy girly fun. Don't hold back.

If you are the honored recipient of more than a couple of showers, try to avoid saying things like: "Oh. *Another* cheese board." "Trivets. Mmm." "It's a . . . a . . . a . . . a—oh, you *made* it?"

During all these festivities, something will have to be done with your fiancé. You can't have him coming in and spoiling the all-girl atmosphere. Being the only male in a room full of half-crocked, squealing women on a sugar jag sounds good in theory, but it's bound to make him squirm like a six-year-old. Find a male friend or relative to take him off your hands. A Charles Bronson movie, a

giant truck rally, a trip to the auto parts store—any of these is a perfect male bonding rite.

Well, it's down to the last few stragglers, the chips are dying soggily in the dip bowl, and those multiple mimosas have started a throbbing right behind your eyes. It's time for you to head out. You gather up all your new precious belongings, but at the last minute your exhausted hostess hands you one more giant box. It's a tradition, after all, to take home your centerpiece, all your decorations, and every last ribbon and bow. After all, even the debris from this event is sacred. Tears will well in your eyes every time you open this box and remember this precious day and all the happy moments. That is, every time every five years or so that you forget what's in that big box taking up all the room in the back of the closet.

7 DISASTER PREPAREDNESS

Look on the bright side:
planning your wedding has
made you eligible for a job
as a corporate dealmaker
and welfare at the
same time.

NATURALLY THE CEREMONY, the very crux of the wedding, is always left to be planned until the last minute. Different clergy have different ways of dealing with engaged couples. Some have a specific rule about premarital counseling. Reasonably enough, they tend to feel bad about marrying a couple they feel are bound for hell. Unless it's your family pastor, priest, or rabbi, though, they don't know you from a hole in the wall, and they think that in one or two sessions they may uncover and remedy some hideous flaws in your relationship. Some may attempt to administer a compatibility test, as though a game of twenty questions is going to tell you something you don't already know. Here are some sample questions:

1. My career is (a) less important (b) more important (c) equally as important as my family life.

2. I consider myself a basically (a) even-tempered (b) moody (c) frustrated person.
3. I have (a) career and personal goals that I set and meet (b) no career and personal goals (c) unrealistic goals that I set and I find impossible to meet.

On top of it all, you know that even if this clergyman *did* unearth some fatal character flaws through these tests, he's probably an incredibly repressed white guy who would never dream of pointing out your incompatability; because God forbid that any unpleasantness occur—that's your business.

More appropriate questions would actually be more like this:

1. Even though I love my future spouse, his/her teeth sucking is something that (a) I find endearing (b) I can ignore (c) will drive me to the abyss (d) will cause his/her death someday and no jury would convict me.
2. My wife-to-be's PMS mood swings are something that I believe are caused by (a) changing hormone levels (b) her wanting to get her way (c) Satan possessing her body.
3. When I think of my future in-laws, I (a) smile and think fondly of them (b) think if we try we can grow to be a close family (c) plan to relocate at least three thousand miles away without leaving a change-of-address.

The Catholic church doesn't fool around. It has designed a prenuptial, or "Pre-Cana" weekend retreat for couples that, according to one graduate, was like a combination of traffic school and frat hazing. In an est-like atmosphere, the couples sit in a room for twelve hours and ask juicy, fight-

provoking questions like who's going to handle the money in your marriage. They require you to fill out what you assume are very personal and private questionnaires; then they make you read them out loud. As if this weren't enough humiliation, at the end they ask you for more donations.

No matter how specifically you indicate the details of the event to your clergyman, no matter how much they smile and nod and agree to a brief, succinct, and moving ceremony with a more feminist wording of the vows, they'll end up doing it *their* way. That means long-winded prayers, possibly some surprise kneeling, and, worst of all, slipping the old wife-cleaving-and-obeying business into the ceremony, which leaves you hopping mad. This is their little joke on you. They know you can't really say anything about it after the ceremony because everyone immediately surrounds you and covers you with kisses and you'd look pretty damn stupid standing there stamping your foot and arguing sexual politics when it's your job to look dewy-eyed and happy.

There are members of the clergy and judges who allow you to design your own ceremony, but this can get pretty dicey. A good hint is if, when dis-

They'll slip the old wife-cleaving-and-obeying business into the ceremony . . .

cussing the vows, the officiant says, "Hey, it's your bag. Don't let it be a trip on you." Or he might close with pronouncing you husband and wife "as long as you both shall dig it." You may think you're hiring a perfectly mild-mannered, dignified judge, but he'll show up in a plaid sportscoat with a tie that reads HERE COME DE JUDGE. With stains on it. Or you may be assured by your judge that the ceremony will take no longer than fifteen terse and to-the-point minutes, but there's just something about a burning August sun that makes him tell humorous stories about his mother and himself, get your name and your husband's occupation completely wrong, and wax nostalgic for an hour. No, it doesn't even matter if your rites are practically an avant-garde tone poem—people who perform weddings flagrantly misuse their power. You let that Buddhist monk/ethical culture guy/New-Age minister talk you into using a nice Navaho love chant, and the next thing you know, he or she is inviting guests to come forward and give you their personal blessings—in the form of sappy poems. Worst-case scenario? An ill-groomed Deadhead cousin steps up with a guitar and a song written just for the occasion. Ouch! These are the kinds of things that will give your guests the impression that this is not the most stable relationship and that one of you will ditch the other soon to go learn to levitate or avoid the ugly consequences of a New-Age pyramid scam. You want classic, you want traditional, you want the kind of ritual that reaches back into the ages? Don't engage someone to administer your vows who will start out by quoting "Eleanor Rigby" and then finish by saying, "Or we could all ask ourselves, 'What's it all about, Alfie?' "

What *is* it all about? Going into bridal over-drive, that's what. And why not? Your wedding is mere weeks away. Other, more organized, more mature, more, well, let's face it, more *anal* brides would have everything under control. Sure, their cakes are ordered, every last one of their groomsmen's tuxes are fitted, their overbearing church wedding directors have been successfully bullied—all done! But you, on the other hand, with the help of your family, your fiancé's family, and all your friends, are on the verge of losing your mind. What major planning concerns are to others are minor last-minute details to you.

Like the seating chart. You suddenly realize that no one but you could possibly do the seating arrangements. Let's face it. Your mother would screw it up, your fiancé could give a rat's ass, and no way are you going to turn it over to the caterer—what does he know about your friends and family and the subtle nuances of their alliances and feuds? The people you work with want to sit with the other people you work with, but not with people they used to work with. Your grandmother's canasta club wants to sit together, except for Esther, whom nobody gets along with. Your single friends without dates want to be seated next to single men—but only good-looking, eligible, successful ones—after all, you're getting married, for god's sake, you owe them. Your cousins will sit anywhere, anywhere except next to Uncle Louie, your brother Dinky, or that guy they met at your last party who wants their number. You're not only expected to plan the invitations, the ceremony, the menu, the music, the mood—you're supposed to become a world-class diplomat overnight. Every single person who said to you, "It's your wedding,

darling. Do what you want," is now insisting that you juggle the entire room so they can sit where they please.

A few weeks before the wedding, someone may tactfully point out to you that, traditionally, the bride hosts a luncheon for her bridesmaids. With everything else you have to do, it hardly seems fair. It would take time away from doing the really important things, like countless shopping trips to narrow down that shoe choice, trying to decide how to wear your hair, and giddily paying full retail prices for your honeymoon clothes. Being told you have to host yet another party just about takes the cake. You're supposed to pay *them* back just for buying a really great dress they can *definitely* wear again and actually getting to participate in the wedding of the year? Hey, what's this whole thing about about—you or them?

Who Does What: Wedding Attendant Checklist

MAID OF HONOR

- hosts not one but three showers for the bride
- has ability to constantly reassure bride that she doesn't look puffy
- will hold diuretic pills for bride
- will inform bride what her less-sincere friends are saying about the impending nuptials.
- doesn't mind spending hours wandering through malls with the bride to look for shoes and discuss vague nuances of heel shapes
- does not become irritated when bride incessantly changes subject from nonwedding-and nonbride-related topics back to wedding-and bride-related topics

- will pour over racks and racks of pantyhouse and commit to memory 106 shades ranging from frosty beige to taupe snow

BEST MAN

- will discuss with groom everything *but* the wedding—sports, weather, babes, sports
- helps groom act like nothing's going to change after he's married, except the ol' ball-and-chain
- plans a bachelor party that ends up, after all, being just the guys driving aimlessly around at 3:00 A.M., just like in high school
- feeds tequila to groom on day of wedding so that he passes out during the first dance (helps if he and the bride hate each other.)

BRIDESMAIDS

- argue amongst selves over choice of bridesmaid dresses
- reassure bride that dress is great and agree with her that you'll definitely be cutting it off and wearing it again
- behind her back, bitch about the bride's choice of attendants' gifts and curse her first-born child
- get pregnant so that the dress barely fits, just to spite the bride
- spend the morning of the wedding soaking all the André labels off the champagne bottles to hide the bride's shame

Reading Between the Lines of Wedding Announcements

Naturally, even though your mother's been nagging and nagging you to see to this one petty detail, you put off dealing with the society page announcement of your wedding until now. Where

you live and in which newspaper you want to announce your wedding will dictate your luck in postponing this little chore. If it's the *New York Times*, forget it. You need to send in your vital stats at least two weeks in advance. On top of that, there's a rumor that they have a "secret point system" that you are judged on to qualify for a couple of taut column inches. It'll inform less about your wedding and more about who both sets of parents are, where their money comes from, what you and the groom do to justify your trust funds to your friends, and where everybody went to prep school. Both family's gross worths are encoded in this information, and if you don't know what the secret point system is, don't even ask.

If, on the other hand, you want to announce your nuptials in a small-town paper—say, the *Petit Jean Country Headlight*, of Conway County, Arkansas—you probably only need a few hours' advance notice so that the society page lady can write a Proustian full page all about your dress, your maid of honor's dress, your attendants' dresses, the groom's, groomsmens' and ushers' tuxes, your mother's dress, his mother's dress, your flowers, your bouquet, your cake, the groom's cake, your bride's book, special out-of-town guests, where you plan to honeymoon—and a full description of every single last party thrown for you since you announced your engagement.

Now which do you think is more in the spirit of the-bride-as-center-of-the-universe? Unfortunately, your mother will still insist that your announcement be published in the city where she lives so that people she hasn't heard from in years will call her up, stop her in the street, and generally treat her like the queen-by-association that she is.

Armed Response

By about a week before the big day, you will have received less than half of your invitation response cards. Panic sets in when it occurs to you that everyone invited will actually show up. You couldn't have made it easier for your guests. You included a card that had boxes for "will attend" or "will not attend." You included a pre-addressed, stamped envelope. How inconvenient could it be for them simply to check it off and drop it in a mailbox? Very inconvenient. You, evil bride-to-be, are confronting two basic human fears. A terror of correspondence and the dread of decision-making. The only way to solve this is for you to call everyone and ask them if they have any intention at all of making it to your wedding. You'll have to spend extra money and extra time to do this, and guess what? They often won't offer an excuse for not having responded so that you can make the elaborate plans for what is only, after all, the most important day of your life. The small percentage who do respond will have scratched out "will" and written "maybe + 5."

And isn't it about time to pick up your wedding dress? After all, you want to allow a little extra time in case the alterations aren't exactly perfect—but you won't. Somehow you'll manage to squeeze your dress appointment into your lunch hour. It's so exciting, so lovely to see yourself in your wedding dress again now that it fits, but . . . something is wrong. You told them you didn't want those inch-thick foam cups put in the bodice, but did they listen? For one thing, everyone knows you're not a D-cup, and for another, after your new husband embraces you at the altar, you'll walk

back down the aisle with concave bridal breasts! You demonstrate, "Look, see?" pushing them in yourself, but the bridal saleslady, Mrs. Stalin, has the audacity to stand there and tell you "No vone vill notice thees." And so a scene ensues, you screaming, your face all tear-streaked and puffy, your breasts pushed in, and Mrs. Stalin with her arms crossed, stalwart in her refusal to remove them—"Dollink, dollink, it vill ruin your lines!" Finally, a manager is summoned, and a compromise is reached: the cups are removed, and you are made to swear on your mother's grave that you will march right out and buy an elaborate, whalebone-laden, circulation-constricting foundation garment to torture your bustline into the dress's shape.

Naturally, you'll want to wait until the very last minute before you take care of the only details that are really critical to your wedding day. One is getting your marriage license; the other is the blood

. . . you'll walk back down the aisle with concave bridal breasts!

test. It's only natural that you've put them off. They're not fun, like choosing your table decorations or what kinds of little mints to have. They're also not a matter for intense scrutiny or endless argument. They're just some of those annoying things the law wants you to do.

With all the money you've been shelling out on deposits lately, the last thing you want to do is pay a doctor's appointment price for a simple test to prove that your bodies aren't wracked with social diseases. What to do? There's always your local community clinic, which offers not only the test at a bargain rate but also an opportunity to mingle with large groups of your contagious community, in a small, airless room. No copies of *The New Yorker* or *Smithsonian* here, but you will have the opportunity to catch up on reading last week's classified ads. Eventually, your name will be called, and your blood will be taken. By someone. Is he a doctor? Is he a nurse? Is he in rehab? Whatever,

. . . you can't help but notice the incredible array of incongruous couples . . .

he's wearing a T-shirt that says, DON'T MESS WITH MY TOOT-TOOT, and his hands are clean, even if his fingernails aren't.

Once armed with your blood test, it is time to proceed to the local bureaucratic hellhole—the county clerk's office. Here the romantic and beautiful concept of matrimony is reduced to dull, witless officialdom. Did I say simple? You may be misled by lobotomized city employees into visiting multiple civic institutions before finally finding the one, correct, endless line in which to stand. Once there, you can't help but notice the incredible array of incongruous couples also seeking to obtain their marriage licenses. Like that short, fat forty-something Bride-of-Frankenstein lookalike with the tall, emaciated prison-tattooed fellow of about nineteen with the slicked-back hair and bad skin. Accompanied by her fifteen-year old son. Or the crew-cut, camouflage-jacketed survivalist and his tiny, non-English speaking, mail-order bride-to-be.

Or the broadly beaming elderly gent with the gal who has the blowsy look of a soon-to-be-ex-show-girl. Do these exotic couplings reassure you of your own compatibility? Hardly. It's long waits in lines like these that start you scrutinizing your own darling extra hard. You never noticed before now how his teeth were extra long, his ears unusually pointed, and how he really just has one eyebrow that goes all the way across his forehead, which is kind of, well, low. Don't worry about these second thoughts. He's thinking the same about you. If you can make it up to the registrar's window without splitting up, you have only to face a dour, loveless clerk whose economy of movement makes a postal employee look like a whirling dervish. By the time you finish with the paperwork, this mind-numbing experience, like a visit to the tax accountant, is a lot more sobering, and final, and real, than your wedding day will ever seem.

8 THE BIG HAUL

"If you have to write a thank-you note for it, it's not worth having."
—A GROOM

A MADCAP, materialistic romp. A gratis, greedy grasp for goods. An unapologetically swinish spree. You'd think you'd be able to enjoy registering for gifts at your favorite enormous department store. But between your husband-to-be, who has regressed to the point of lying down in the aisle and sobbing, "Mommy, I'm s-o-o-o-o bored!" and trying to decide if it's worth going back up five more floors just to pick out a goddamn clock radio, you've got a throbbing headache. Obviously, bringing him along was a big mistake. But along with that is the realization that, because you set up housekeeping some time ago, you don't even want or need 75 percent of the stuff you're allowed to register for. Add to this sullen clerks, malfunctioning bridal registry computers, and your groom's disappointment that they don't have an automotive department, and your consumer fantasy is shot straight to hell.

I think cash is the most sentimental gift of all.

However, people with no taste seldom agree with this. They want to give you something special and unique that will make you think of them each and every time you use it. And you will think of them—at your garage sale. Those buying you gifts feel they have the right to ignore your bridal registry list, your taste, and your personality, and choose what *they* feel are the correct totems of Gracious Living.

When you pay for the wedding yourself, you're setting yourself up for disappointment. You figure you should get some pretty great stuff, because to you, your wedding is like your birthday, Hanukkah, Christmas, Valentine's Day, Easter, and Halloween all rolled into one. To everyone else, it's either just another annoying obligation to shell out for, or an opportunity to express creatively how they feel about you. Either way, you're going to get many things so ugly you can't even look at them. You'll receive dishes made to hold extinct foods like aspic. You'll feel like an idiot when you actually do use that crystal wine carafe that is suspended from a wrought iron stand. Surrounded by these new belongings you will start to feel less like the hip thing you are and more like someone who has had a subscription to *Woman's Day* since she

was three. Years from now, people will be able to pinpoint exactly when you got married because your everyday china will look just that out-of-date—and you will have picked out the pattern yourself.

You'll be overwhelmed by the sheer number of multiples. Apparently, most of your guests assume that being married means drinking a lot of fluids. The largest percentage of your gifts will be tumblers, tankards, flutes, steins, goblets, wineglasses, ice tea glasses, shotglasses, rocks glasses, juice glasses—every imaginable kind of drinking vessel. The marvelous thing about this is that, if you like, you can put off doing dishes for a few years. The second-most given gift seems to be picture frames, every last one an 8″ × 10″. You may get dozens of them, and guess what? No one will think to give you the grand piano to match. Never mind. With your crumb whisk, toast rack, chafing dish, and candelabra, you can still pretend you're Leona Helmsley.

The bridal industry toils twenty-four hours a day to manufacture the most dazzlingly ugly wedding chotchkes they can think of, so don't be surprised if a few of these things surface in your home. From personalized cake knives and toasting glasses to padded satin-and-lace wedding video cases, from a suction NEWLYWEDS ON BOARD sign and mugs that say things like BRIDES ARE SPECIAL PEOPLE to matching T-shirts that say EAT YOUR HEART OUT, I'M MARRIED, you'll discover a whole new level of bridal barbarity.

Be prepared to have your entire living space transformed into a landfill. The sheer volume of boxes, wrapping paper, and packing material may force you to start your own recycling center. Don't

be surprised if, during this intensive gift period, while at work, you must excuse yourself because of an uncomfortable itch. You didn't know styrofoam peanuts could work their way up that far, did you?

You'll make one new friend—the lady at the returns desk at the department store where you registered. The onslaught of gifts will send you back there time and time again because of things you just don't need, just don't want, or have multiples of since the bridal registry screwed up so badly. The returns desk lady has the painful job of telling you just exactly how much your sister-in-law-to-be paid for that coffeemaker. She'll be able to tell you which gifts, in their decaying original boxes, haven't even been made for thirty years. She'll even be able to tell you that the "Visions" cookware you can't seem to return anywhere in town is sold exclusively through the Home Shopping Club.

To top it all off, you can't complain about any of this stuff, you ungrateful little cow. You're just supposed to be lucky that people thought enough of you to give you all these lovely, lovely things.

Some day, after all this is over, you'll find yourself in conversation with another recent bride. You'll be dying to dish the dirt to *someone* about the incredibly tasteless array of bad wedding presents you both got. How you saw that big, blue Tiffany box and thought you were getting some massive, classy, ultimately exchangeable expensive thing that turned out to be a microwave bacon rack. What moxie, huh? No sympathy here. After all, when she registered for that Baccarat crystal, she thought she might get, at best, one or two nice pieces. Imagine her surprise when one of her entertainment lawyer husband's friends presented them with the entire set. Then there was the shock of discovering another pal had paid for the whole honeymoon. Oh—one bad present. A really very minor, very inferior Picasso etching . . .

Gift Checklist

GLASSWARE ACCESSORIES

- 13 cheap cut crystal bowls
- 12 sets of champagne flutes
- 17 sets of assorted drinking glasses
- 11 sets of wine goblets
- 8 matching beer steins
- 5 ice tea glass sets
- 1 Waterford rocks glass
- 9 relish trays
- 4 decanters

SERVING PIECES

- 17 serving trays
- 3 bed trays
- 4 tea trays
- 2 cake plates that double as punch bowls
- 5 deviled egg plates
- 7 chip-n-dip bowls
- 1 silver-footed fruit dish
- 23 baskets
- 7 thermal carafes

HOME ELECTRONICS

- 1 dancing flower
- 1 electronic "annihilator" noisemaker for the car
- 1 smoked lucite and brass grandfather clock

HOME APPLIANCES

- 1 electric apple peeler
- 3 electric bun warmers, one in original box from 1973
- 4 salad shooters
- 5 chafing dishes
- 2 indoor barbeques
- 2 Frydaddies
- 3 percolators
- 1 pressure cooker

DECORATIVE ACCESSORIES

- 1 hideous "rain" swag lamp
- 3 lamps that would look good in your grandmother's house
- 9 sets of candlesticks
- 3 candelabras
- 1 needlepointed pillow that has your wedding day stitched into it
- 1 handmade quilt, completely handstitched—made of 100 percent polyester doubleknit
- 2 brass horsehead bookends
- 1 wall clock embedded in Jesus-in-a-picture-frame
- 1 swan guest towel holder

- 17 picture frames
- 8 indefinable ceramic receptacles for rubber bands, loose screws, pennies, pencil nubs, and old Q-tips

LUGGAGE

- 13 matched pieces in brown-and-orange faux-vinyl moc croc

HOMEMADE GIFTS THAT SHOULD HAVE GREAT MEANING BUT SIMPLY INSTILL GUILT

- 1 gold-glazed ceramic tea set w/service for eighteen, made in your aunt's ceramics class in the hobby shop at her trailer park
- 5 laminated wedding invitations, two with burned edges for that "antique" look
- 1 hanging macrame bath towel rack
- 1 hand-embroidered picture of two ducks on a lake—from your uncle
- 1 needlepointed *TV Guide* cover

INCOMPREHENSIBLE GIFTS FROM PEOPLE WHO SHOULD KNOW BETTER

- 1 plastic Richard Nixon shower head
- 1 tiny stuffed penguin made out of fur
- 1 used teapot, with a broken handle, three chips, and dried blobs of spaghetti sauce on it
- 1 used, broken vase

- 1 silver three-pronged thing—you don't know what it is
- 1 candelabra-ish pewter Swedish thing
- 1 picture frame engraved CONGRATULATIONS JUDY AND JIM

9
GOOD GROOMING AND YOU
Two on the Aisle

IT IS TEMPTING to think of your husband-to-be as just another bridal accessory. It may be easier for him to play along with this too. After all, you don't expect your shoes or your beaded bag to help you make decisions. Bridal magazines suggest that he's avoiding the entire issue because he feels left out. You've only to make him understand *how much fun* it is to register for flatware, study nosegay styles, and obsess over the choice of rice or bird-seed *together*. Once he grasps the giddy gaiety of it all, *then* you can treat him like a formalwear store dummy. You may have to pay and pay for reducing him to mannequin level for as long as you both shall live—but that's *after* the wedding. So relax, enjoy—this is your moment.

Don't burst into tears when he says he doesn't care what your theme colors are. This apathy is not uncharacteristic behavior for him. What's in this wedding deal for a guy? It has to do with everything men hate: dainty food, polite conversation, dancing with elderly women, and lifelong commitment. You could sock him with the ol' teary-eyed "Maybe you don't care. Maybe it's not the most important day of your life." Of course,

then he'll have to listen for a few seconds, but do you really want him to? Once he knows you want to stuff his pals into pink tuxes (you said pale apricot, but he fails to see the distinction), you'll get *involved* with a vengeance. What your man wants is veto power—the right to say no to everything. Relax. It doesn't matter if you go ahead and do everything anyway—he just wants to make a stand.

Men don't want to know all the millions of details. "Big deal," they say. "Order a cake, buy some flowers, get a guy to take pictures." They think it's just that basic. They will not sympathize with the pressure you are under to bring the Most Beautiful Day of Your Life to full flower. "So what. So you couldn't find mauve mints." Their concept of good food for the reception is ribs, burgers, or chili. They had no idea, until now, that you would fight to the death to defend tiny wedding cuisine that looks and tastes like cute refrigerator magnets.

By now, since he knows he can't possibly win, your groom will start to sense a strange conflict between feeling excluded and not wanting to know anything. This kind of confusion, along with being confronted with polaroids, diagrams, and lists on a daily basis, can make your special guy feel completely powerless. Spell that E-D-G-Y.

It's only normal to expect that your relationship will undergo growth, adjustment, and change, while you plan, together, for the most beautiful day of your lives. Your fiancé is growing tired of adjusting to the fact that, overnight, you've changed into a banshee. When he comes home to find the floor littered with bridal magazines, bubble wrap, and honeymoon package brochures, while you and your bridesmaids are glued to the TV tipsily studying a video called *French Braiding Magic*

while drinking mimosas, he'll wonder what happened to that carefree, beer-drinking girl he used to know and love. Reassure him that you're still that girl, but does he think you should register for *both* the crystal champagne flutes *and* the champagne saucer glasses?

The Bachelor Party—Not to Worry

Even though your beloved claims that you, and only you, bewitch, bother, and bewilder him, he'll be-watching X-rated videos in a motel room with the guys. This is a male-bonding session with a vengeance, boys only, drinking, smoking, and lying their asses off. Now this is exactly the kind of thing that seems a little too personal and perverse to you and me to be a *group* activity, but, for the boys, communal viewing of the naked female form is a form of, well, fellowship. In other words, it gives grown men the prepubescent thrill of getting away with something really, really naughty. Not to worry. Usually, you'll find that

. . . you and your bridesmaids tipsily study a video called "French Braiding Magic" . . .

the friend in charge of the event will feel that actually *organizing* a bachelor party is too fruity a thing to do, so he'll wait until the last minute to suggest casually that the boys all come over for a few beers and, uh, er . . . take it from there. Here's what this means:

- Everyone convenes at best man's house.
- Beers drunk for approx. 1 hour.
- TV turned on.
- Channels flipped until an old black exploitation movie, *Coffey*, is found on cable.
- Many comments and suggestions made re Pam Grier's breasts.
- More beers are drunk.
- Lull in conversation when Pam Grier's breasts no longer on screen.
- Suggestion to go to strip joint met with rousing approval.

At the Baby Doll Lounge, one of your fiancé's more innocent friends is uninformed as to go-go lounge etiquette—i.e., buying a watered-down,

. . . for the boys, communal viewing of naked females is a form of fellowship.

overpriced drink for a scantily clad dancer who engages you in conversation while on her break. He chats away, telling her all about the groom, his lovely bride-to-be, and how they met, ignoring her look of impatience. Finally he asks, just to be sociable, "So, do you work here?" and she replies, "No. I just like to come down here and hang around in my bra!" and storms off.

Those less innocent may just do what men do in these places: get wasted and watch the real thing, up close and personal, howling, hooting, and screaming for more. That is, until something like this happens: one of the senior strippers is notified that a member of the audience is about to lose his bachelorhood. She takes it upon herself to offer sex tips to the guest of honor by demonstrating on stage, all matter of factly, while chewing gum. ("Hon? Lissen. Okay, do it like this—are you watching? This is important. *Not* like this.") This is bound to be interpreted more like a National Geographic Special on primal tribal rites than a triple X classic by your fiancé's more, er, sensitive pals. Soon, your shitfaced-but-fascinated darling will find himself standing alone. Then he'll wander outside and find the others sitting in the car, where the topic has switched safely to sports. Along about 3:00 A.M., they'll wend their way to a White Castle, and the worst you have to fear is a hangover, raw onion breath, and beautiful memories.

WHEN TO WORRY

There is the rare occasion when your fiancé's best buddy is a truly thoughtful, creative, and Eddie-Haskell-like sociopath who will mastermind a one-

way trip to the Island of Lost Boys for your beloved and all his friends. This is the kind of epic saga about which you really want to know nothing. Unless his friends do something like get him drunk and dye his body red from the waist down, or shave the same area, you won't really *have* to know anything. However, painful little snippets will make their way back to you in veiled comments from his friends, like, "Babe, you've got nothing to worry about. Twenty pounds of silicone can't compare to the real thing," or, "and then she screamed, 'Take it out! Take it out!' " (followed by raucous laughter). This is the kind of base, primal escapade that you assumed your beloved was incapable of, the kind of low experience he'd turn up his nose at, the kind of adventure that movies starring Tawny Kitaen are made about. Just remember this: when you are forced to solicit your out-of-town guests for spare cash to bail out all the male members of the wedding at 5:00 A.M. on the Most Beautiful Day of Your Life, it will become a legend in the annals of your family history, a story everyone will laugh about later. Everyone but you.

10 ENORMOUS CHANGES AT THE LAST MINUTE

The Rehearsal Dinner:
Or, the Hatfields and the
McCoys Meet over
Roast Beef

WHAT BETTER WAY to purposely construct stress for yourself than to take part in yet another social event the very night before your wedding? Gather both his family and yours, add the members of the wedding party, your clergyman, and the clergyman's deaf, elderly mother, and god knows how many out-of-town guests who've arrived early and invited themselves, stir well, and serve.

Count on someone in the wedding party being late to the rehearsal. It could be the minister, it could be the best man, it could even be the groom, setting up all kinds of suspicion to percolate amidst your relatives. Even when he does show up, five minutes later, does it allay their skepticism? No, they're merely disappointed that they don't get to witness personally your betrayal at the hands of this unknown fiend—not yet, anyway. With your clergyman and that incredibly bossy wedding director lady do-si-do-ing everyone through the steps, the rehearsal starts to feel more like a square dance and less like a wedding. You'll get the feeling that nobody really understands their motivation. Then you'll ask that everyone study their script and rehearsal notes, which you whipped up and made copies of in a neurotic organizational frenzy this morning at 4:00. You'll insist that it be done again—maybe just five or six more times? You'll be roundly laughed down. Have you figured out by now that everyone but you is just marking time before they get to chow down on some free eats?

There's no such thing as a free rehearsal dinner. Even though, technically and etiquette-wise, his parents foot the bill, you'll pay and pay. Don't think his mother hasn't been fretting about her responsibility for this event. If it's even possible, she's been more obsessed than you, probably because she's only had this and her dress to plan, instead of a million details to oversee, like you. So you'll go into overtime reassuring her. Yes, roast beef will be fine; yes, everyone likes mashed potatoes. Yes, sherbet was a good choice for dessert. Yes, it's okay that they don't serve liquo—what did she say? No liquor? Did you think things seemed edgy at the rehearsal? That was because everyone was dying for a drink. Now it'll seem like a madcap romp compared to this.

Sometimes, the rehearsal dinner is the first place

120

the parents of the bride and groom get a chance to meet—and what place could be more appropriate than the florescent-lit banquet room of a low-priced chain restaurant? Everyone sits at a long U-shaped table so that it's only possible to talk to the person on your right or left, or stare at unknown persons eating far away, on the other side of the U. Watch the interfamilial tensions build, build, build across the banquet table. As the ice starts to break, just a little, the favored topic of conversation among the men is, in depth, the route taken from their hometowns to here. "We stayed on 440 all the way to I-95, then we swung south on 67." "You could've taken 805 further north, you know . . ." Even without the benefit of alcohol, you can count on certain voices to carry, precisely at the moment there is a lull in this scintillating chitchat. Usually what is said is something very loud, along the line of ". . . buck-nekkid nigra standing right outside my patio door!" All heads turn toward your cousin from Texas, who blithely continues her story without missing a beat. Everyone will chalk one up for the groom's side. Even if there is liquor served, everyone is watching everyone else so intently that no one has more than a glass of two—which hardly takes the edge off. God forbid they should get tipsy and blurt out something like your cousin just did. No, your loved ones will save the opportunity to get com-

pletely blasted for tomorrow, the most beautiful day of your life.

You'll excuse yourself to powder your nose and find your maid-of-honor hot on your tail, dying to dish about his relatives. In the ladies room, as she rattles on and on about his Aunt Phoebe's incredible beehive do or his dad's enormous honker, she doesn't seem to get that your dagger looks, wild hand signals, and whispered hisses of "*Ixnay! ixnay on the ossip-gay!*" indicate a spy from the other side in the next stall. If you're lucky, she won't address you by name, and you can escape unrecognized.

Finally, much, much later, you're safely tucked away in your prenuptial sarcophagus. This doesn't mean the partying has to stop. Au contraire! Your wedding is a microcosm in which anything can happen—especially when all your out-of-town guests are in one hotel. In the course of twenty-four hours, new drink recipes are discovered, total strangers become mad, passionate lovers, long-term relationships collapse, emergency rooms are visited, bail is made. Worse, in this time, they'll develop their own set of in-jokes, obscure references, and a whole mythology about the groom's and your behavior. In perspective, I think it's lovely that years from now, your old pals will be arguing still about whether your new husband deliberately pitched you into the band's drum kit while dancing to "Brick House" or whether you just "lost grip."

Oh, by the way, the evening of the rehearsal dinner is deemed the correct time to present each member of your wedding party with a traditional thank-you gift. After all, they've spent time and money to help make your wedding vision com-

plete, so the least you can do for them is give them a small remembrance. I hope you're ready. Don't think you can get away with unloading extra stock your dad, the wallet company representative, has been storing in the basement, or your mom-the-Avon-saleslady's free samples. These people know you. The books suggest "timeless and simple jewelry," but lockets, bracelets, and keychains have been done to death. Just how much are you supposed to spend per gift, anyway? No one has a good rule of thumb for that. Is four bucks too little? Could you get away with ten? No? What do they want from you? Did someone say something about pearls? Are they supposed to be real? You're already in debt up to your bridal eyebrows. (Don't take the risk of trying to recycle your wedding gifts now. People tend to look askance at items engraved with your names and wedding day.)

Just when you're past the point of caring, the innovative wedding industry always has new ideas. Add insult to injury (they paid good money for those oh-so-unflattering dresses and tuxes) with a tacky plastic double picture frame with your wedding invitation on one side, and a clock on the other. The clock face is a bride-and-groom silhouette that says, OUR LIFE TOGETHER, and will remind your girlfriends of you for years to come—each time they try to unload it at their garage sales.

What about the men? Avoid aftershave and cologne like the plague. Men who would actually use the stuff should never be encouraged. There's always that manly monogrammed something. Belt buckles and money clips are okay, but lighters and hip flasks aren't. Keep in mind that boys will be

boys. On the most beautiful day of your life, the boys may get drunk and giddily try to set each other afire.

The Fine Art of Worrying

Those who take seriously the pursuit of needless anxiety should consider less pointless fretting about mere petty realistic concerns and instead concentrate on world-class idle fidgeting: things that are highly unlikely and yet still just barely within the realm of possibility. Savor the deliciousness of not possibly being able to predict or control these things. And what's more heart-stopping fun— sweating over things that could actually happen, or the kind of worrying you do when you wake up from a nightmare and still think it's real? Are you a mere amateur fussbudget, or an angst Olympian? Try these wedding worries on for size:

- Someone will stand up and say why this union should not take place—and it's because the groom is actually already married and has fifteen children.
- Your hair could catch on fire as you walk down the aisle.
- Your dream about being naked at the altar could, conceivably, somehow, happen.
- Everyone you invited could actually show up.

Even under the most ideal circumstances, where everyone agrees that you *should* be completely in control of all of the plans and you actually *are*, as the wedding day draws near, the smallest of minute details will be blown far out of proportion—for example, whether to order an extra corsage for

Aunt Beverly, who isn't in the wedding party, but feels she deserves one, whether the "something old" that you'll be wearing as a bride is old enough, or whether to serve regular sugar cubes with the coffee, or those ones that break in two. Count on it: you will have the ugliest of screaming fights with someone near and dear to you over one of these issues. It's times like these that can make you spontaneously combust or just ditch the whole thing at the last possible moment and elope.

Get the Ladder!

Whether you decide to go downtown to City Hall, fly to Hawaii, or drive to Las Vegas and tie the knot, elopement will offer lots of surprises. Spontaneity is its own reward.

After waiting patiently, at a town hall in some quaint burg, behind some people who are getting a permit to burn trash, you can file for a license. Naturally, you'll be pleasantly surprised and delighted when, along with your marriage permit, you're presented with a complimentary gift. The romantic bubble may burst outside, on the street, when you open the gaily colored tote bag to discover a small can of Edge shaving cream, a mail-order coupon for Frederick's of Hollywood, and a container of Massengil disposable douche.

Disposing of that, it's on to the justice of the peace's. These places, more often than not, can be slightly less than you hope for, decorated by those same people who do bail bondsmens' offices, with dusty plastic ferns, cheap paneling, and outdated calendars. One of the reasons you may have chosen elopement was to avoid the entire issue of

being judged by others. However, don't be surprised if this still happens—perhaps in a more subtle way. For instance, during the ceremony, when the j.p. gets to "If there are any among you who see why this marriage should not take place, speak now or forever hold your peace," he might conceivably pause for what seems like *hours*—even though the only people present are you two, the j.p., and his wife, the witness. After receiving no divine interdiction, you may eventually get to say, "I do." It's kind of sweet.

If that doesn't sound romantic enough, there's always Hawaii. Imagine tying the knot in a tropical setting. Sounds dreamy, right? The dream probably doesn't include a judge who bitterly bitches at his wife, in charge of snapshots while he performs the ceremony. After snatching the camera away from her and taking the pictures himself, he tells you he can only hope that your marriage will be as happy and as full of contentment as his has been. P.S. His wife's roll of film turns out perfect. The judge's cuts off your heads.

But why go all the way to Hawaii when you can have an experience even more bizarre? Of course, I'm talking about Las Vegas. All the greats have been married there. Elvis. Barry White. Kitten Natividad. Why not you? It couldn't be easier or more simple. This is Wedding Central. If you call the Las Vegas tourist bureau 800 number, they can give you all the information you need about where to get your license and how to reserve a chapel. There are dozens, with names like the Candlelight Wedding Chapel, Mission of the Bells, the White Lace and Promises Chapel—although personally I'd feel a little odd about getting married in a place

named after a Karen Carpenter song. The downtown Las Vegas wedding license bureau is open twenty-four hours a day to serve your wildest impulses. Two o'clock in the morning, when you're tired and groggy after a long drive, is a great time to drop by and check out the variety of other couples who had exactly the same idea you did. Three in the morning is even better for going to the chapel, which really should be called a *gift shop/ chapel*. As you wait for the minister to arrive—he's on call—you'll be able to make almost all the same decisions you have been agonizing over for months—in just a few moments! There, you can buy your rings, your garter, your veil—even rent or buy a dress! Choose between silk or real bouquets,

corsages, and boutonnieres. Choose between live music or pre-recorded music. Choose a photo package. Choose what song you want. Choose your ceremony, religious or nonsectarian. Buy the video, or just an audiotape of your wedding. But wait. There's more. Why not buy your *own* wedding gifts? After all, by eloping you'll have to send back the ones sent to you by people who expected to be at your wedding. Buy picture frames, lingerie, mugs, ashtrays. Tell the world with a button, postcard, or license plate frame that says I WAS MARRIED IN LAS VEGAS. What could commemorate this experience better than a baseball jacket with the name of this chapel on the back? Don't look now, but the minister is here, and he's ready to go. So what if he has a speech impediment that makes him sound like Sylvester the Cat, and so what if the gift-shop clerk who just sold you that peekaboo bra is doubling as the witness? It's just as meaningful as if you had gone through with those Big Plans, right? Besides, instead of having to hobnob at your ho-hum reception, you can spend the rest of the night playing the slots.

One bride I know told me that Las Vegas seemed to her that night more beautiful than Paris, and her bridal suite at Caesar's Palace had a golden glow about it. Not only that, but all the schmaltzy love songs that were playing on the casino's loudspeaker were suddenly filled with great meaning. Anything can be romantic. It all depends on your point of view. But if you've given actual *thought* to these options instead of just acting on the impulse, you'll know it's way too late to elope now.

11 THE BIG DAY

*"I take you to be my
waffly leaded husband"*
—A BRIDE

EVEN IF YOU DON'T spend the eve of your wedding carousing with your old buddies and are deep in sensible slumber, someone should have the good sense to wake you at four in the morning so you can be Too Excited to Sleep together. Sisters are always good for this. This is the time for happily regressing into girlhood, rehashing old arguments—"You're the bossy one." "No, you are." "No, you"—and playing beauty makeover fifteen times. It's moments like these that make sisters extra-specially close—that is, unless she's older than you, not doing so well, and has chosen this particular morning to confront you with all that anger she's been working on lately with her therapist.

Maybe you're not a typical hand-wringing, face-clawing, cold-footed bride-to-be. Perhaps you got plenty of sleep, and you didn't wake up with a throbbing in your temples and your mother staring at you funny. Maybe you feel perfectly calm. You've got catching up to do. Pitch yourself head-first into the hysteria of your wedding day!

Insist that while you are getting ready, there be *at least* thirty other half-dressed people in the bridal antechamber to watch, advise, comment, document, rave, sob, smoke, pass out, eat, nurse, and deplete the ozone layer with thirty-seven cans of hairspray. You want to be in a party mood. Have you practiced your glassy-eyed bridal stare? You can't get married without it!

By today, your sacred vow will have become a huge joke. I'm not talking about love, honor, and obey. I mean that promise you made to yourself to be a size six for just one day. This would mean that years from now you could show those wedding pictures and say, "Yes, I always was such an itty-bitty thing." If all went according to plan, everyone, even your husband, would come to believe that this was so. He would've even bought into the fantasy and added wistfully, "Why, I could put my hands around her waist and touch my fingers together." But no. Because of all your nervous prenuptial noshing, your mother will have to safety-pin you into that perfect Miss Junior Petite wedding dress. She'll tell you for the four thousandth time that "You're just big-boned, like me," and you will be mean to her because you're so hung over, and she will cry. This is the point at which you realize that you, too, have become just an accessory for your dress. Look at it this way: if it's one of those weddings where people pin money on the bride, now there's more square footage to cover with bills.

It is traditional to allow your mother to bear the brunt of *all* your anxiety, especially if she's been a perfect saint through all this, because she knows that moms are for blaming. But don't expect her saintliness to hold up indefinitely. All that guilt

tends to implode, and even the mildest mom can turn into an unrecognizable harpy from hell. You'll recognize it by that look in her eye. It's that same strange look she got when you were fifteen and you came in at 4:00 A.M. after being out with your really really cool hippie boyfriend Che. Remember: when you push a mom over the edge, anything can happen.

Mom, in her heightened state, will start to make demands. If you're lucky, she'll only want to Scotchguard your dress—after you've put it on. "Cover your eyes, honey!" But you just don't know. Even if she's been a good sport up until now, she could suddenly offer to get you out of this whole deal. "I'll tell you what—instead of getting married? Let's you and me go shopping!" You might be innocently applying your makeup, when suddenly she appears over your shoulder, squinting hard into your magnifying mirror. "Oh my god!" she'll exclaim. "You have giant black hairs growing out of your chin! Shave them off this instant!"

. . . your mother will have to safety-pin you into that perfect Miss Junior Petite wedding dress . . .

Flipping over to the unmagnified mirror side, standing under natural light, and calling it "a little peach fuzz, Ma, c'mon" only makes her scream louder. Now she's waving her ancient Lady Schick in your face, and you realize you won't get out of this room alive unless you do something. Slap some Nair on and scream back, "Are you happy now, Ma? Happy?" and be done with it.* In any of these instances, you'll want the wedding videographer there to get it all on tape, so that later, when she denies her psychotic behavior, you'll have proof.

ON THE NUPTIAL NOD

Before the wedding, there's a good chance that everyone will want to force drugs on you. They're completely wigged out—shouldn't you be too? Even if you are, remember: Valium won't just "relax" you. It'll put you in a kind of bliss-coma. You may be happy, but you won't know why. It'll wipe out the most beautiful day of your life. Did you plan this elaborate rollercoaster ride for months and months so that you could be unconscious for the thrills, chills, and spills? If anyone offers you a happy little capsule, suggest that they take it. They'll probably be grateful.

Gilding the Lily

It's time to gather your muses about you to make of you a vision of unearthly loveliness. Not one, not two, but three fussy gay professionals will be just right to do the job: your hair, your makeup,

*That is, until your honeymoon, when you actually will have giant black hairs growing out of your chin, from using Nair.

132

your floral headpiece, and your nerves. Just as one puts the finishing touches on your hair, another steps in to re-create your face through the magic of makeup. Then the hairdresser will have to suffer through watching the florist destroy his panorama of perfection by poking it full of flowers. He'll have to step back in, touch up, mousse, gel, spray, and blow dry, smudging your makeup and wilting your flowers as the other two wince and sputter. Then the makeup artist will have hover, dab, and pat, hover, dab, and pat, until all is restored. The florist will replace flowers. Back and forth they'll go like this, until the hairdresser accuses the florist of using your head as a vase, the florist points out that it was an ugly vase anyway, and your makeup man complains about their enormous clumsy hands. And you thought you got to be the queen today.

The photographer will more than likely want everyone assembled immediately before or after the wedding for group pictures. Organizing everyone to be in one place at the same time, twice in one day, even with pastel-colored limousines to get them there, is no mean feat. Doubtless, the picture location you yourself suggested is a bosky dell—where it has recently rained. All the gals' high heels sink instantly into the ground, soiling their dyed shoes and sending them reeling like weighted Bozo punching dolls. With you and the photographer doing your best to keep everyone on schedule, your voices are growing shriller and shriller by the minute. Best men and ushers have a tendency to disappear for long periods to perform bodily functions associated with too much alcohol. Ringbearers and flower girls are guaranteed mud-magnets, and someone, usually a mother, will not stop cry-

ing. If your location is a public place, people will stop and gawk. If you're still in the drinking marathon that started last night, then now, when you see your reflection in that little eyeshadow compact mirror, is the time for regret.

Perhaps you just couldn't resist the urge to be photographed in a horse-drawn carriage. Strangers' hands have been all over you, fluffing your sleeves up, smoothing your skirt down, spilling your cathedral-length veil artistically out of the carriage, and spreading it out on the lawn. Your mother has climbed in and wedged herself between you and the groom to touch up your hair every five seconds until it's three feet higher than it started. You've been blotted, brushed, rouged, and dabbed until you thought you'd scream. Finally, you are perfect. The photographer is just about to take the picture when the noble steed decides to relieve his bladder—all over your train. Don't worry—later you'll treasure that candid shot the photographer got of you throwing your bouquet at the horse.

Here Comes the Bride

The moment has arrived. Naturally, since you were the only one paying attention during the rehearsal, you are now certain that everything will go wrong at the altar. Every possible permutation of what could happen will now flood your mind. There's always the chance that your fourteen-year-old cousin bridesmaid has just chugged a couple of rum coolers that one of the ushers sneaked in, and as you hear the first three notes of the wedding march, she will turn to you and say, "Gee, I think I'm gonna be sick." More likely, though the members of your wedding move like cattle,

they'll probably all get up the aisle okay. Your toddler nephew and niece ringbearer and flower girl, on the other hand, will do their best to sit down halfway, pee, cry, and steal the scene. It's frustrating, but remember—the crowd is eating it up.

If you're lucky, after Dad deposits you, he won't suddenly hesitate about whether or not to sit next to your mom, whom he hasn't seen since the bitter divorce twenty-two years ago, or on the other side of the aisle. Once you're in place and the clergyman begins his familiar drone, your wedding party will start to get distracted. It's not hard. Unless it's your wedding (and sometimes, even if it is), even the most fascinating and articulate man of the cloth is just about the easiest person in the world to tune out. Especially if he's added a few extra invocations he neglected to tell you about, which he most assuredly will. While he's reading from his prayerbook, it's okay to sneak a peek at that cute guy standing next to you. The almost indiscernible act of eye-rolling can help reduce a lot of tension, although if you're holding hands, you can pretty much judge his nervousness by the zeal with which he's milking your fingers.

Despite all the hope in the world and last night's little "Getting to Know You" get-together, you can't expect that the groom's and your families will fall in love with each other. The reason tradition has his and your tribes sitting on opposite sides in the church is so that they can identify each other. This way, your aunt can make catty remarks about that pronounced underbite that seems to run in the groom's family. His cousin can safely express her opinion about your bridesmaids' dresses. All this, right behind your nuptial back. The best you

135

can hope for is the very essence that binds families together—that each side will secretly reassure one another that the other really doesn't know how to behave.

Looking idly out at the crowd and calculating how long it is before they get to chow down, your bridesmaids will have taken on the expressions of grazing cows. Your maid of honor may be so distracted that you'll catch her offguard. You may have to wave your bouquet in her face to get her to take it and hand over the ring. This is the point at which you actually have to tune in to what the person marrying you is saying, because you have to repeat it. Don't say, "Huh?"

The ring passage itself is always awkward. Nervous brides and grooms have even been known to simply hand each other the rings instead of putting them on each other's fingers. This beats trying to jam it on a by-now swollen digit while repeating what the clergyman says all at the same time. This doesn't sound hard, but the phrase "With this ring, I thee wed" doesn't exactly roll off the tongue. The combined effort can seem a little like juggling

flaming meat cleavers. To help you out, the groom may subtly wiggle the correct digit at you. This is his way of saying, "Psst! Honey! Over here!" while you're desperately trying to zero in on the moving target. Your frustration could cause a foot-stomping bickerfest to spontaneously combust right then and there. Don't let it happen. It'll all be over pretty soon; then you get to make out in front of everyone and grin like monkeys as you skip back down the aisle.

If it isn't entirely a blur, in your first few moments of married life, you may notice people, especially family members, crying. Is it the overwhelming emotion of this important life ritual that moves them to tears? Are they touched by the way love has transformed you into a dewy-eyed beauty? Well, of course—but some of these are also tears of relief. After all, certain relatives took it for granted that, one day, you'd be found dead in a motel room, naked but for a tube top, a lawn chair and a beer cooler your only possessions. And worst of all, still single.

You'll pass by a table at the entrance to the

Tribes sit on opposite sides of the church so that they can identify each other . . .

reception where a white ostrich-plume pen and guest book have materialized, seemingly out of nowhere. An elderly female relative you recall only vaguely has been given the job of making sure every single guest signs it, and even now has some chum of yours in a boney vice-grip. Don't try to rack your brain remembering when you discussed this particular detail with your mother. You didn't. But that's okay. All mothers and their friends belong to a secret wedding army reserve that is ready at a moment's notice with an arsenal of plume pens, white leatherette-bound guest books, and enough white lace tablecloths to cover the earth. And guess what? You've just been inducted.

Reception lines, like communism, sound good on paper. You may enjoy being hugged, kissed, and given warmest wishes by your first twenty-five or thirty loved ones, but the novelty will begin to wear off—especially if, further down the line, you find yourself in an intimate clinch with an elderly, overweight man with denture breath whom you've never seen before in your life. This is the gauntlet you must run in order to get to that first glass of champagne, which you'll need pretty badly by now.

Usually, the best you can hope for in the toast is a heartfelt speech that includes worshipful and poetic praise for your beauty, grace, and ability to redeem that no-good low-down skunk of a guy the best man has been proud to know. But it's rare that anyone ever chooses his best man on the basis of his toasting ability. No, erudite best men are few and far between. In fact, you'll be lucky if your groom has even informed his best man that making a toast to the new couple is one of his unconditional duties, so at the very moment all your guests

are gathered for this tribute to you, the best man may be nowhere to be found. Finally, he'll be drummed up, lipstick on his cheek, hair tousled and his shirt rumpled, a panicked look on his face as he launches into an impromptu speech: "Ah . . . well, ah, uh, may your marriage last as long as our friendship, man. . . . No! Longer!" And that's the kickoff.

Don't expect your reception to be like any other party you've ever been to. You'll rarely have enough time to finish a sentence before you get dragged off to talk to someone else. Out of the corner of your eye, you'll witness money discreetly being slipped to your new husband like it was . . . well, like it was a payoff. Never mind that. It's all like a dream anyway—not that naked-at-your-finals-dream, no—the dream you have where everyone you've ever known has gathered in one room. Wow, there's your uncle flirting with your mother-in-law! Look, it's your new brother-in-law talking to your old college boyfriend! Hey, wait a minute . . . over there, it's your grandmother talking to the guy who used to sell you pot in high school! Freaky! Just as you're being approached by your girlfriends, five or six or seventy elderly people block their way and surround you. Be kind. Remember, these people have come to watch you do this big thing, and they've all brought you wonderful gifts, like ceramic teddy bears that dispense Kleenex, so they deserve just a few minutes of your time. Over their heads you can see your mother telling an amused group of your co-workers about the time you peed in your Tweetie Bird Halloween costume. While you're shouting small talk to someone who was old when you were in kindergarten, you'll overhear the best man informing your rela-

tives that your new husband is actually a bag boy at the A&P. It's going to take a lot of work to dispel that little joke, but later, because now you're being dragged on yet another round of picture-taking. Did you want to be queen for a day? Well, this is how royalty earn their pay. Gladhanding, diplomatic smalltalk, and paparazzi. Don't expect to see much of your new husband today, because he'll be busy doing the same thing. Does the food look good? Forget it. Every time you try to take a bite, someone will take your plate out of your hand so you can be fawned over properly. You'd think actively masticating food would ward off kissers, but you're wrong. You'll be kissed by people who are themselves in the act of chewing food. You'll be hugged by people juggling plates who come this close to spilling stuffed mushroom caps down your front. And you're never too old for some relatives to pinch your cheeks. Hard.

Even the most well-organized wedding planner cannot predict the incredible things people will say

You'll be kissed by people who are themselves in the act of chewing food.

on your wedding day. These things fall into two categories: momentous advice, and completely inappropriate comments. You'll forget the advice, but the inappropriate comments will stay with you until the day you die. The groom's grandmother may observe that your younger cousin certainly looks nice. So nice, in fact, she may outshine you. Your new sister-in-law might decide that this is the perfect time to discuss the possibility of the groom's same grandmother moving in with you two. Your uncle, married to your mother's sister, may decide to take the groom aside and let him in on a little sexual advice. "Sonny, I know the secret of the women in this family," he'll whisper. "Baby powder. Drives 'em wild. I keep a gallon-size by the bed." Your new husband will probably be too taken aback to ask him if he's done field trials. Your mother may feel the urge to tell your new husband's great-aunt how proud they are to have him in the family, but be surprised at her snappy comeback: "Well, of course, we don't know a thing about your daughter." Your devoutly Catholic grandmother may snidely mention that your distinctly nonsectarian wedding looked like a seminar. And your own mother may shout out to you as you're having a group picture taken, "Honey? Baby! Keep your head up. Because when you look down? It shows your third chin." *Third* chin. Thank you, Mom.

What about those who find it so unbearable that you, and not they, are the center of attention? You may start to notice them and their antics—like your cousin with the enormous hat and veil that cover the hives she's broken into as a result of not being the queen today. And then there's that guy whose first words to every female at your

reception have been "Hope you brought your diaphragm." Your stepsister's lowcut strapless dress and frantic dancing style have resulted in a pool being started by your ushers and the band about just when her breasts will be making an appearance. Don't worry. These pitiful stabs at spotlight grabbing can't take anything away from you. How could they? You're wearing the biggest dress in the room.

Of course, as the Bride, you will be kept up to date by others about things you'd probably just as soon not know. Different friends will report back to you about the oddest things. For example, "That sax player with the band is really something." "You know, that sax player said the funniest thing to me—he said he was crazy about my shoes." Finally, the bigger picture will emerge. "You know, that sax player asked me what size shoe I wore. Then he asked for my phone number." This, from your aunt? You finally get a glimpse of a strange little man who looks like Harry Dean Stanton sitting up on the bandstand. He waves at you. What? The band takes another break, and he walks over to where you're chatting nicely with your grandmother and the minister's wife. "You're really beautiful," he says. Huh? "Maybe it's just that *bridal* glow," you offer. "No, you really are. What size shoe do you wear? You wear high heels a lot?" The bandleader comes over. "Hey, Raoul. I was just outside. Who's the chick sitting in your car?" "Oh, man. That's my girlfriend. She's gonna be mad at me. She's been sitting out there since four o'clock. Hey"—he turns back to you—"can I get your phone number?" It's stories like this that will, believe it or not, make your wedding day.

Sometimes, parents will decide that documenting their daughter's wedding is more important than the event itself. This bride will remember nothing about her wedding because she was outside the reception hall the whole time getting picture after picture taken. The same kind of parents tend to hire very aggressive videographers who will mercilessly hound the guests, hovering over them with floodlights at the dining tables. You'll know that your video team was too dynamic when later you see closeup footage of your sweet old auntie, floodlights in her eyes, ranch dressing on her chin, screaming, "No, no, no! This is my meal! I don't want to say anything to the bride and groom!"

If you decided, instead, to have a friend with a camcorder handle everything, try to make sure they don't try to get too "arty." Sure, they may ignore the corny "video tribute," in which guests are all asked to say something nice to the bride and groom. But they may opt for something more . . . interesting. Like asking everyone, "So, you think the bride and groom will stay together?"

Of course, minor disasters may come up. You might hand that fistful of checks people have given you to your grandmother to hold—and by the time you get back to her, she's forgotten whom she handed them over to. A little nerve-wracking game of twenty questions may ensue. "Grandma, what did he look like?" "I don't know, he had red hair. . . ." "There's no one here with red hair, Grandma." "Oh. Well, maybe it was brown." "Was he tall?" "You know, it might have been a girl—a girl with short hair . . . or was it long? I think she was wearing a red thing." You'll have to leave the mystery-solving up to someone else, because right now, you've got to cut that cake.

Cake-cutting is an annoying little ritual that the photographer almost always insists on. Why, why, why do they have to get that picture of you and your new husband awkwardly holding the lily-of-the-valley-laden cake knife* as you look idiotically into the camera? The cliché is almost too unbearable, but one little flick of the shutter, and there you are, tritely immortalized. As if that weren't bad enough, you can never talk them out of that stupid cake-feeding routine—because a cake-smooshed face is a photo opportunity dream come true. Well, never mind. You've just made all the little girls at your wedding very happy. They can finally find something else to do besides hang around the cake.

Of course, now what they're going to do is hang around you and pester you until you finally throw that bouquet. Your jaded, too-cool girlfriends will race off to the ladies' room the very second your overexcited aunt announces this event, leaving those little girls competing only with each other, and your sister, who will wrench it from their tiny hands. You happen to know this is her seventh bouquet catch.

By this stage of the game, any kind of control is out of the question. Your wedding has taken on a life of its own. Since you're either still a nervous wreck, exhausted, or out of your mind with goofball happiness, it'll be hard for you to tell if other

*Courtesy, again, of the secret wedding army reserve.

people are enjoying themselves at your wedding.

Here are a few clues. Despite your screaming insistence that a good band couldn't possibly be found for under a thousand dollars, that all-Philippino octet your mother hired for $650 really has people jumping. In fact, the crowd's gone wild. Speaking of wild, when newly paired-off guests vanish for a while and then suddenly reappear with foolish grins and disheveled clothing, you'll just have to assume that they, too, will treasure memories of this day. When you overhear your new WASP mother-in-law gasping to your mother, "If I'd known dancing the hora was this much fun, I would've done it at my wedding!" you'll know *she's* definitely entertained. And, later still, when dancing styles start to seem less traditional and veer into the largely impressionistic, when that elderly, fragile-looking man your bridesmaids were initially hesitant to dance with has completely worn out every woman in the room, when you see your normally dour grandmother giggling like a schoolgirl, there should be no doubt left in your mind. Finally, when just about everyone has collapsed at their tables, and they're tired but they still don't want to leave because they're watching the last two people out on the floor twirling, not with each other, but with their champagne glasses, well, then you'll know that you've done things right.

12 POSTNUPTIAL LETDOWN

Are You Donna Reed Yet?

AS YOUR NEW HUSBAND woozily staggers across your wedding night threshold with you in his arms, it's quite likely that sex is the last thing on either of your weary minds. Don't worry. Even if you are one of the few, rare virgin brides on the face of the planet, everyone else can tell you that wedding night sex is highly overrated. After a tense and emotional day of meeting, greeting, and drinking, you feel about as much like having a highly charged Ultimate Erotic Encounter as Mother Teresa. That hubby of yours, if he hasn't passed out already, is probably grateful that you're not playing the role of a panting biker chick from a Motley Crüe video. Relax. Order up a VCR from room service and unpack those movies you thoughtfully rented in advance. Snuggle up and watch *The Incredible Mr. Limpet* or *The Shakiest Gun in the West*—because there's nothing like Don Knotts to get your mind off sex. That can wait until the morning, or the rest of your lives. You've got a license to do it now.

Going back to your parents' house the morning after your wedding to open every last one of your gifts is probably not your idea of how to start your honeymoon. Daddy, however, paid that obnoxious video guy for the whole package deal, so he insists. And guess what? Using that married woman status thing just does not wash with these people. Hung over and still tired, you'll dutifully collapse on the couch and start ripping. Later, you'll watch in shock and dismay as a more haggard-looking you than you've ever seen takes all the strength she can muster to tear bridal wrapping paper off gift after gift. Meanwhile, your mother, offscreen, demands that you say what everything is, who it's from, and read aloud every single last card. Dad is busy playing Cecil B. deMille. "How come you're not smiling? That's a nice gift! Act happier for the camera, honey!" Later, everyone but you will find your video interpretation of Hallmark poetry hilarious.

The Not-So-Grand Tour

Your wedding is not the only event in your life that will be rife with overblown expectation. Just like your reception couldn't be just another party, your honeymoon can't possibly be just another vacation. It's just *got* to be a more perfect romantic montage of champagne suppers, panoramic sunsets, and long wordless walks on moonlit beaches than any turgid romance novelist could ever dream of.

There is something about honeymooners, adrift as they are in a world of heightened expectations, that makes them far more vulnerable to disaster. Airline strikes, cancelled flights, flying during electrical storms, lost luggage (and along with it, birth control), hurricanes, sunburn, tropical diseases, sullen natives, incomprehensible road signs, and overpriced food—all these will happen more to newlyweds than to anyone else. Still, you will press

on, determined to have a good time even if it kills you, or you kill each other.

God forbid your honeymoon is the first trip you two have ever taken together. Any couple who is even remotely considering marriage should be given a road map, a rental car, and two weeks alone together. Now, *that* is a compatibility test. Sure, you think sharing in discovering new places, native customs, and quaint and colorful locals will leave you both with treasured memories. But no. Travel with the one you love is only a tool for hammering out the bickering template for your life together.

At some point on your honeymoon, the man you married will not ask directions. You will keep insisting that you're going in the wrong direction to get to the attraction/museum/restaurant/store/ landmark that you are sure is only going to be open for fifteen more minutes. He'll disagree. Once you finally reach this destination, open or closed, it will have fallen far short of your expectations. This is the moment at which you will discover the

This is the moment at which you will discover the Point of Honor.

Point of Honor. There will be a spat over just who it was who wanted to go to this place so badly in the first place, just who it was who wouldn't even stop to ask directions, and just who left the critical information behind in the hotel room. This spiral of disagreement is potentially endless, since both of you are at fault, and neither one of you will back down. The Point of Honor will be invoked time and time again mainly because both of you have such an exaggerated idea of your Perfect Honeymoon that each of you can't believe the other person is acting so much like . . . well, so much like him- or herself.

THINGS THAT WILL BE SAID
ON YOUR HONEYMOON

- "I didn't go on my honeymoon to spend three hours in an outlet mall!"
- "What do you mean *I'm* the one who wanted to see roller-skating cockatoos?"
- "Oh—like I was supposed to *know* that Myrtle Beach fills up with drunk college students on Spring Break?"
- "We're supposed to climb sixteen flights just to get a holy medal for your aunt?"

It's your honeymoon, but how could you possibly feel like making love? You've been in organization mode for so long now there's no stopping you. Your scoutleader mentality has taken over. Your new husband complains that you're distracted during sex, and you are. Instead, you're thinking about if you'll have enough time the following day to see two museums and a play and find that romantic little restaurant your girlfriend Roberta insisted you eat at. Also, your highly recom-

mended "cute 'n' cozy" hotel room is only six inches wider all around than the bed itself. Since there's a heatwave and no air conditioning, you're forced to keep the windows and the drapes open, and crawl across the floor to avoid exposing yourselves. Sure, you're wearing that sexy negligee—you packed it, didn't you? But you won't be flattered by your husband's appreciative stares. "Just because it's our honeymoon doesn't make me a sex kitten!" you'll snap.

It's not like there won't be precious moments. You'll drop your husband in front of the hotel, thinking you see a nearby, convenient parking space. Instead, you'll suddenly find yourself hopelessly lost in a maze of forbidding, dark, narrow streets that only moments ago seemed quaint and charming. Forty-five minutes pass like forty-eight hours before you finally find your way back to the hotel. Your poor husband has long since passed the point of annoyance and is tearing his hair out, sure you've been kidnapped by third-world terrorists. A tearful reunion will ensue. Romantic? Well, sort of.

Day after day, you'll pass the other Americans in your hotel lobby, sobbing about their tiny rooms. But you've learned to adapt—you're on your honeymoon, after all. For your last night of newlywedded bliss, you splurge and enjoy an exquisite meal, a bottle or two of fine wine, celestial desserts. After a romantic walk on a lovely night

"Just because it's our honeymoon doesn't make me a sex kitten!"

150

back to the hotel, you discover the elevator has broken down. Who cares? You're young, you're in love, you can climb five flights easy . . . on the smallest spiral staircase you've ever seen. After just one flight of going in constant circles on a stomach full of cream sauces, sugar, and alcohol, your husband pants, "Don't . . . worry . . . honey . . . I'm right . . . huh . . . behind . . . huh . . . you!" This is when you realize that, should you take one more step, centrifugal force will bring your dinner up and out—right behind you. Is it time to go home yet? Nausea and those thank-you note anxiety dreams you've been having say yes.

Even if you had a wretched time on your honeymoon, you must learn to put it in the proper perspective. As you catalogue for others the terrible wrongs done to you, a picture of your honor, courage, and enduring love in the face of honeymoon hell will emerge. And remember: as a newlywed, you still have a kind of sacred aura about you, so they have to listen.

Returning from your wedding trip, you'll start to get on each other's nerves as you regale friends with tales of your travel. "Sweetheart, you're telling it wrong. The German peed out the window at four in the morning, not midnight." "Darling, if you tell *that* story again, I swear I'll scream." "Honey, Aunt Mamie doesn't want to hear about Yugoslavian toilet paper." Soon it will be easy for everyone to see that you've made the adjustment to married life.

Let's Go to the Videotape

How fortunate we are to be living in the electronic age. What was only a blurred memory to our par-

ents and even our older siblings can now be analyzed, rewound, and scrutinized frame by frame, over and over. Of course, there are disadvantages, too. If video hadn't captured the precious moments of your ceremony, you'd never have known that the groom's combover blew straight up in the breeze, so that he resembled a bald rooster, and that by trying not to cry you actually looked like you were smirking. You'd certainly never have known that your sister-in-law was chewing gum all the way through the ceremony. You'll have sudden, blinding flashes of wisdom: how there is no way in hell your bridesmaids will *ever* wear those dresses a second time. Of course, you're a bride, not a filmmaker. How were you to know that the videographer would make the entire tape a tribute to your maid of honor's breasts, using them as a kind of touchstone from the beginning until the end of the entire event?

Watching your wedding video will be like getting a grip on an accident, where everything just seemed to happen so fast. Relive those awkward moments of the ceremony, like when your dad didn't know he was supposed to sit down next to your mom, even though they've been divorced ten years, so he spent the whole time on the wrong side of the aisle, expressing his embarrassment by scowling and biting his lip. Replay in slow motion the zoom-in closeup of the whopping cold sores both you and your betrothed managed to develop that morning. Realize, for the first time, just *how* long-winded your minister/priest/rabbi/judge really was. As sacred as your vows were, after the second or third viewing, you'll be fast-forwarding through this part to get to the good stuff—the reception.

The first shock you have to get over is your own

bad self—like how big your hair was, how your dress kept slipping off one shoulder, and how you walked like a marine in those heels. You looked like a fairy princess, and that's just all there is to it.

Not until now did you realize just how much you missed by being the center of your own universe. This video is almost like being there—as a guest! You'll see things you couldn't possibly have caught otherwise. Watch, rewind, and watch again as your uncle (who never was quite right after the war) repeatedly takes full glasses of champagne out of elderly relatives' trembling grips, down them in a single gulp, and replaces them in the old folks' hands. Observe, for the first time, how your ex-boyfriend has brought a total bombshell date and they're making out on the video—yes, for your benefit. Notice that the exact moment the rabbi closed his mouth after the blessing of the meal in Hebrew, the band launched into "It's Now or Never." (Also, later they played "Will You Still Love Me Tomorrow?") You'll come to the realization that older people sometimes have a home-movie mentality about the video camera. They assume there's no sound, so you'll find them later on in your video, looking like complete fools as they wave and make exaggerated toasting gestures, saying, "Don't worry about me! Just ignore me! I'm just doing this for the camera!" These are the unique moments that make your wedding video special. Of course, there are bound to be a few moments that you could have done without. After all, you've seen your mother chew food before. And chew. And chew some more. Of course, you've seen your own rear end before too—but never in a big white dress while bending over.

The whole idea behind the "video tribute" is that you would have a lovely document of every last person at your wedding giving you all their warmest wishes on this, the most important day of your life. In truth, there's nothing like a camera pointing at tipsy people caught offguard to make them freeze up, hem, haw, waffle, and generally act like they're being threatened with cattle prods. There is, however, something very touching about your grandmother, with an expression combining concentration with fear, saying, "I want to congratulate Susan and my new grandson, Jennifer," as someone, off camera, whispers, "Jonathan!" "Who's Jonathan?" The voice whispers, "Susan's husband!" Your grandmother says, "Oh." And smiles.

You'll be so fascinated by your video that you'll watch it time and time again. You'll insist that everyone you know, even if they were there with you, relive, rewind, and rewatch the magic. For anyone who had the incredible misfortune to miss what now, in your mind, was just the best wedding in the whole wide world, it'll be mandatory viewing—if they expect to leave your house alive. When folks politely remark that watching it was almost like being there, agree wholeheartedly, and tell them where you're registered. You've got to prolong your queen-for-a-day status as long as you can.

Picture This

Of course, mere magnetic tape is not enough to put the most beautiful day of your life into perspective. When you lovingly pour over the photographer's proofs, you'll discover details too subtle for videotape, captured for all eternity on film—like

the bridesmaid unsuccessfully cupping her cigarette, the smirking teen usher with his hands on his crotch, and that soggy lunch bag on the grass in the foreground with the decaying sandwich spilling out. You'll wonder why anyone would make the effort to get him- or herself into every single table shot—usually someone you're none too fond of. Naturally, you'll treasure all the pictures taken throughout the day of your mother—even if her bra strap is showing in all of them. Of course, you'll have no idea who that woman in the semi-transparent dress is—but you can't guess why she ended up in so many of the pictures.

When the photographer announced he wanted to shoot the immediate family in your parents' living room, your mother was so hot for an elegant portrait of her clan that she went into a frenzy clearing all the ugly stuff out of the way and tossing it into one corner. Of course, the light was best in *that* corner, so the hideous Don Quixote figurine, that Mediterranean swag lamp, and an overloaded electrical outlet are just over your shoulder in every shot. You could, as some people do, reassemble everyone and have the pictures re-shot—but wouldn't that be cheating, like those TV news shows that present "crime reenactment" as the real thing?

No matter how much you insisted, you weren't able to talk the photographer out of that stupid, bizarre, double-exposure shot that has you and the groom in the background worshipping the closeup of you in the foreground. Uncomfortably enough, it has captured the gist of what this whole thing has been about—the deification of you, the Bride, by you, the merely mortal couple. Still, you'd just as soon it weren't so tackily obvious. Somehow, though, it got in the contract that you have to buy one. Don't worry. Your grandmother will order a print in the largest size and proudly display it in her den, where it will fade nicely over the years.

The time has come to have your dress professionally cleaned and preserved. Forget that subconscious fantasy you've been harboring about wearing it around the house when nobody is around, because your dry cleaner will admonish you to never, ever, *ever* open the hermetically sealed casket—uh, box with the plastic window. Preserving your dress will feel a little like you're having a beloved family pet stuffed. Is that the symbolic end to your glorious reign, a form of therapy, a way to put your wedding to rest? Not really. You'll be milking it for months yet.

. . . you weren't able to talk the photographer out of that bizarre double-exposure shot . . .

You Little Ingrate

Your family is collapsing under the scandal. Why, it's a miracle they can still hold their heads up in this town. Your father's name is Mud. Your mother's reputation as a mother is ruined. Everyone on your new husband's side is narrowing his or her eyes into little slits and gleefully squealing, "I told you so!" The people who lovingly raised you might as well throw themselves into the river and why? *Because you didn't start on your thank-you notes the moment after you said "I do"—that's why!!!* I suppose you're lazing on a chaise longue right now, blithely nibbling bon bons, thinking this is all very funny, but let me tell you, missy, it's not.

If no female relative has started this tirade already, let me be the first to remind you that many of your older kin have nothing better to do than to count the hours that pass until they get a gushing, gracious, handwritten little mis-

sive from you. And it's not just them. There's just something about that big white dress that just naturally makes everyone assume that you're well-brought-up enough to sit down and personally write hundreds of thank-you notes. If you think just because you live in the computer age you can get away with programming your PC to spit some out, you just think again, madame queen. Every grateful little message must be penned by hand on ugly gift stationary with the same ostrich-plume ballpoint your guests used to sign the white vinyl-bound memory book. You might be able to get away with some duplication, but keep in mind that all elderly female relatives will compare and contrast the notes you have sent them. If you think you can skip a few, you'll be guaranteed to get a phone call from your new mom-in-law reminding you that she ran into Sylvia at the market and she just happened to mention that she still hasn't heard from you.* No, there's no getting out of this.

Your reign as queen is grinding to a halt, heralded by the fact that no one—including your new husband—will volunteer to help write your thank-you notes. And no fair hiring anyone else to do it. But here's a tip—buy the tiniest little thank-you cards you can find so you don't have to write more than a few sentences. Of course, it would be lovely to write everyone effusive, chatty, ten-page letters that include details about just how special their presence made your wedding and multiple witty anecdotes about the honeymoon and that reiterate in what a personal way you'll be using their thoughtful gift every single day—but it's just not possible. You'll switch, soon enough, to the pithy-and-

*The secret wedding army reserve is keeping tabs on you.

to-the-point correspondence school. People don't ask for much. Four sentences will do.

1. Apologize for the length of time elapsed before the note was written (even if you're writing them on your honeymoon).
2. Thank them for the gift and describe how you will think of them every time you use it.
3. Either tell how much their presence at the wedding meant to you or regret their absence.
4. Beg them to stay in touch.

Just make each and every last one unique and special, that's all.

While you're soaking your writing hand, you may find yourself doing a little postnuptial soul-searching. Was it all worth it? Family and friends may join with you for a while in reminiscing about the golden moments of Your Day, and reinforce your belief that, indeed, it was the best wedding ever. But the year's grace period that applies to wedding gift-giving and thank-you notes, you'll discover, does not apply to your reign as Bridal Princess. Within only a month or so of your wedding, loved ones will start to get a distracted look in their eyes and gently hint that the subject has been exhausted: "Shut up already. "Get a life." "If I hear one more word, I'll scream!" Take these as clues.

You'll have to find some other way to fill your

*Every grateful message must
be penned by hand . . .*

I GROSS
THANK
YOU
NOTES

hours, now that you can no longer command the attention you found so thrilling, so satisfying, so right. Learn to entertain at home. It's important to have any kind of gathering in your home during the early days of your marriage, just so that you can put to use your new mammoth array of trays, coasters, and relish trays. And, for a perfect melding of your new domesticity, the showcasing of your acquisitions, and your recent addiction to the spotlight, start a newlywed support group. Let's face it, other new brides are the only segment of the population left with whom you can bask in the dying glow of your aura.

Newlywed Support Group Activities

- Pour lovingly over one another's wedding albums and videos while secretly confirming that your wedding *was* better.
- Get out your grudge file and discuss the wrongs done to you by others during your reign as queen.
- Compare and contrast who got the best and worst gifts. Secretly resent those who made out better than you.
- Plan a wedding-gift garage sale with other recent brides; then come to the conclusion that not only could none of you risk the possibility of gift-givers actually showing up, but also no one would ever buy what you're trying to get rid of.
- Discuss how your friends and relatives now planning their weddings don't seem to value your opinions and advice.
- Above all, take turns listening to one another drone on and on about those pre-wedding

glory days of sanctioned self-indulgence, the guilt-free shopping, the endless searches for just the right shade of pale pink nail polish. Wistfully reminisce about the way family and friends would patiently confer with you for hours about the tiniest of pointless details. No one else wants to listen now. You're just some old married broad.

Wedded Bliss

At first, referring to that guy who used to be your "boyfriend" as "my husband" feels as odd as that new ring on your left hand. The first few times it comes out of your mouth, you won't be able to believe you said it. To call him "boyfriend" indicates youth, vitality, romance—like Marlo Thomas, That Girl, squeaking perkily, "My boyfriend, Donald." "My husband" seems matronly, almost haughty—until you discover the power it wields with chauvinist tradespeople. Sometimes trying to assert your autonomous right to good service may just be wasting your time and energy. That's when you trot out "My Husband." As in, "My *Husband* will be *very upset* when he hears about this." They're just sexist enough to assume your husband is a three-hundred-pound linebacker who'll rip their heads off if they don't get the spot out of that jacket/fix the car's alignment/install the air conditioner right away. It's simply amazing. In reality, My *husband* is probably just an average repressed guy who avoids confrontation at all costs. That's why it's up to you to bring out the big guns. Who said being married wouldn't be fun?

Now that it's all official, many people seem to have absolutely no qualms at all about asking you

if you're pregnant. If they don't suspect you *had* to get married, they assume you've gotten started. They won't even ask if you're trying. First they'll be coy. "Are you, ah . . . ?" "What?" you'll say. "Have you . . . ovulated yet?" "Excuse me?" you'll reply. That's when they'll cut to the chase. "How's his sperm count?" If you wear anything in the least bit baggy around your husband's parents, don't be surprised if your new mom-in-law takes you aside and excitedly asks, "When are you due?" This is when it occurs to you that being pregnant might be a way to keep that spotlight from fading to black. Yeah, maybe that's it. . . . You'll be damn lucky if, just at that moment, someone else's two-year-old bursts in, makes any possibility of adult conversation impossible, and destroys the room in 3.3 seconds. No, perhaps you should just retire the bridal crown and experience domestic bliss before you produce an heir to systematically destroy life as you know it.

Now that you've come to your senses, a terrible worry will cross your mind: did your wedding really have deep meaning for only you and your beloved? Was it just a silly, shallow party for everyone else? Of course not. A Major Life Event is never without repercussions. Now that you're an Old Married Broad instead of a fairy princess, you won't be spared one link in the chain reaction set off by your nuptials. The only people left who'll want to talk about your wedding are the ones victimized by it. First, your thirty-four-year-old single girl-friend will call up, not to ask how your honeymoon went, not to see how you're settling in, but to tell you that Eduardo, the headwaiter at your reception, tried to seat her at your table because he thought she was the mother of the bride! She still hasn't gotten over it—and somehow, you're to blame. Then, of course, your best friend from high school will phone, sobbing that her boyfriend has a new girlfriend—*your* college roommate. Where'd they meet? *Your* wedding. *Your* fault. Worst of all is when your own mother finally decides to inform you that the lovely family heirloom bracelet that Grandma impulsively gave you to wear as your "something old" at the wedding was supposed to be passed from mother to daughter—not granddaughter. Of course, there's nothing your mother could possibly do to ever please her mother, so why should this be any different? It's not like it's your fault, and yet it's *your* fault.

A few of your single friends are definitely faulting you for leaving their ranks. You still enjoy their company, but things aren't quite the same since you lost interest in swapping horror stories from the dating trenches and bitching about how rotten all the men in the entire universe are. Since you two now officially come as a unit, you'll find yourself thinking maybe you should socialize with other units. Finding the perfect Ethel 'n' Fred to match your Lucy 'n' Ricky is not as easy as it sounds. If you're friends with the wife, your husband is bound to think her husband's a jerk. If he's friends with the husband, his wife may bore or even frighten you with talk of cleaning products, coupons, or household hints. Even if you all do get along okay, a movie might be all right—but what if they ask you over for dinner? This could be a potentially endless nightmare—the spiral of obligation. Dinner parties are nerve-wracking. Cooking for four is a lot harder than cooking for two. I mean, you can't eat in front of the TV if *they* come over. You definitely can't bicker in front of *them* about who's going to hold the remote control and who's going to run out to the store for dessert. After dinner's over, you can't just take off your clothes and . . . well, why didn't Donna Reed ever seem to have this problem?

That Donna fantasy you were entertaining about married life just doesn't seem to be panning out. Even in pajamas, your hubby doesn't look a bit like Carl Betz. He still looks just like that cute boyfriend you used to have. And you haven't discovered any new compulsion to wear heels and pearls around the house. No desperate urges have overwhelmed you to spend your days making jello salad, coconut cake, and curtains out of nylon net. You haven't given in to the dull predictability of couple socializing. Your friends still come in uneven and interesting numbers like ones and threes. So now you have to ask yourself: just what has changed since you experienced the rite of passage that was your wedding? Aside from the months you've spent recovering from being queen for a day, you've managed—despite the Tupperware—to emerge with your hipness miraculously intact, a few new appliances, and—oh yeah—a dreamy guy to spend the rest of your life with.